Sketching Cats

Sketching Cats

FRANK J. LOHAN

CB
CONTEMPORARY
BOOKS
CHICAGO

Library of Congress Cataloging-in-Publication Data

Lohan, Frank.
    Sketching cats : pen and pencil techniques / Frank J. Lohan.
       p.   cm.
    Includes index.
    ISBN 0-8092-4059-9 :
    1. Cats in art.   2. Pen drawing—Technique.   3. Pencil drawing—
Technique.   I. Title.
NC783.8.C36L64   1991
743′.6974428—dc20   91-16774
                                          CIP

Published by Contemporary Books, Inc.
180 North Michigan Avenue, Chicago, Illinois 60601
Manufactured in the United States of America
International Standard Book Number: 0-8092-4059-9

To Boots, Shadow, Mittens, Whitey
. . . and Chester

Contents

Introduction

When it comes to cats, people generally have one of two predominant attitudes. There are those who love all cats, or a particular cat, with unreasoning devotion. And there are others who cannot understand such love for an often aloof and sometimes disdainful animal. This book is for those of either persuasion who want to express their fascination with these magnificent wild or domesticated animals by drawing them. It is for anyone who wants to see how easily members of the cat clan, from various places in the world, can be drawn and how much fun it can be to draw their often beautifully patterned forms with either the pen or the pencil.

My primary approach in this book, after discussing the necessary fundamentals of the tools, materials, and techniques of drawing, is to show you how to see the geometric structure of all feline bodies, be they house cats, alley cats, bobcats, or those larger members of the family that are found in Africa, the jungles of South and Central America, and the North American West. I do not go into cat anatomy but illustrate the geometry of cats' bodies by simplifying them within boxes and lines. If you get this geometry straight on paper, it is easy

to "stretch the skin" over it and have a reasonably accurate rendition of your cat subject.

If you have a fair grounding in drawing, the first few chapters will present little that is new to you, but you should at least read Chapters 2, 3, and 4 to become acquainted with the terminology I use in this book. Those without a good bit of confidence in their present stage of drawing development should read Chapters 1 through 5 and actually do the step-by-step lessons presented there as preparation for completing the lessons in the later chapters.

Each lesson in the book includes a list of necessary tools and materials and a gridded outline of the subject. You can use the grid system described in Chapter 2 to easily copy each outline on your composition paper, work it over until the major details look right, and then transfer it to your final paper for completion with the pen or the pencil, according to the step-by-step instructions.

In Chapter 15 you will learn how to draw some animals that are "related" to cats only by a syllable in their names— the polecat and meerkat.

1
Tools and Materials

Pens

Inks

Pencils

Erasers

Paper

Fixative

It does not cost much to equip yourself to do the lessons in this book because inexpensive pens and pencils (as well as more expensive ones) are readily available. If you are not sure that you will have a long-lasting interest in drawing, buy the less expensive items such as the crowquill pens, which have replaceable nibs, for your ink drawing and use wooden drawing pencils. These pens and pencils are more than adequate to produce first-rate drawings and will cost no more than a few dollars. If, however, you intend to draw seriously for years to come, you might want to consider purchasing the more expensive technical pen and/or the artist's fountain pen, which are easily portable and convenient because you do not have to dip the point every few strokes as you must do with crowquill pens. Mechanical pencils, drafting lead holders, and drafting leads also offer advantages over the wooden pencils.

The clerk in your local art supply store can show you all of these items and can tell you how to use and care for them.

Pens

Crowquill Pens
Crowquill pens are the old standbys. A crowquill is inexpensive and has the benefit of taking any of several inexpensive nibs that vary widely in degree of flexibility or stiffness. The stiff ones do not allow much variation in line width, but the more flexible ones spread as you apply pressure to them, producing often desirable variations in line width. The pen holder and nibs look something like those shown in figure 1–1, and produce lines like those shown in figure 1–2. Any India ink or colored ink can be used with the crowquill pens.

Technical Pens
Technical pens resemble the pen illustrated in figure 1–3 (the brands may vary in appearance but their function is similar). The point is tubular and each size makes just one line width. If you want a narrower or a wider line, you must change points or change pens. The points start at size 00000, or 5✕0, a very fine point, and go up to sizes that produce quite broad lines. A happy medium, and the size I use most frequently, is the 000, or 3✕0, although I also use 5✕0 and 0 sizes from time to time. Various sizes of screw-in points are generally available for these pens. I have a complete pen for each point. A number are sold in the fifteen- to eighteen-dollar range; others go for higher prices. CAUTION: Use only an ink that has the words "for technical pens" on the box or bottle. Heavily pigmented India inks, which are great for crowquill pens, can badly clog the fine tubes in technical pens. Buy your ink at the same place you buy your pen to be sure of getting the correct ink container—probably a spout—to fill the pen's reservoir.

Typical line work produced by technical pens is also shown in figure 1–3.

Artist's Fountain Pens
Artist's fountain pens resemble the pen shown in figure 1–4. Like the technical pen, this pen has the advantage of portability and accepts various sizes of screw-in points. In addition, it can produce a variety of line widths from one point, depending on the pressure that is applied. These pens range in cost from

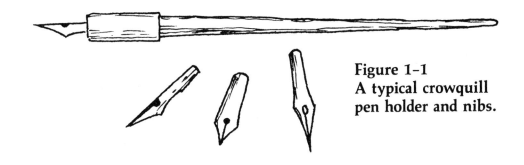

Figure 1–1
A typical crowquill
pen holder and nibs.

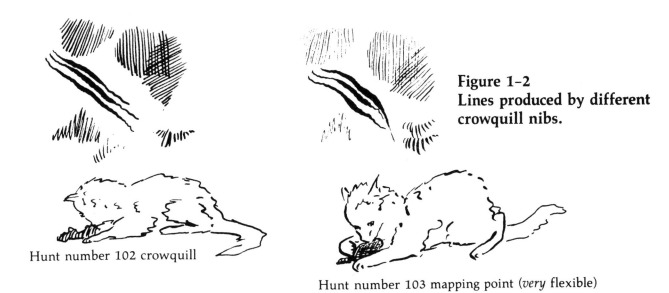

Figure 1–2
Lines produced by different
crowquill nibs.

Hunt number 102 crowquill

Hunt number 103 mapping point (*very* flexible)

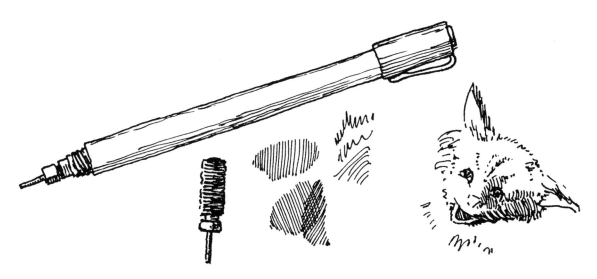

Figure 1–3
A typical technical pen and the kinds of
lines it produces.

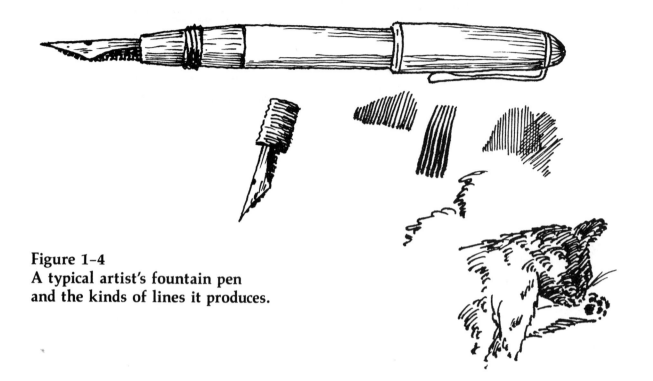

Figure 1-4
A typical artist's fountain pen
and the kinds of lines it produces.

about fifteen dollars up to hundreds of dollars.

Typical lines produced are also shown in figure 1-4.

Inks

There are many different drawing inks available, any of which can be used with the crowquill pen. Technical pens, however, with their fine internal tubes, must have special ink to prevent the tubes from clogging. Ink for these pens (with the words "for technical pens" on the box or bottle) should be purchased at the same time as the pen to insure compatibility and to insure that the proper filling device is provided by the ink container. Technical pens often have little plastic vials to hold the ink, which require a spouted ink container to fill them.

Artist's fountain pens should be used only with ink that is recommended for them.

Pencils

Wooden drafting pencils that you sharpen with a knife and sandpaper, shown in figures 1-5 and 1-6, are the usual pencil-drawing tools. Because of their convenience, drafting lead holders might be used, although they are not absolutely necessary for the beginner. Each holds lead of a particular degree of hardness, such as 4B, 3B, or HB. I use mechanical pencils with 0.5 millimeter leads (very fine leads) in the B and HB hardness for sharpening up the edges of some of my sketches.

The wooden pencils are sharpened with a knife and sandpaper block (the latter is available at art supply stores) so that they look like those shown in figure 1-6. Notice that the flat part of the lead makes broad marks and the sharp edge makes very fine lines.

Whatever pencils you choose to use, make sure that you have leads of 4B, 3B, B, and HB hardness.

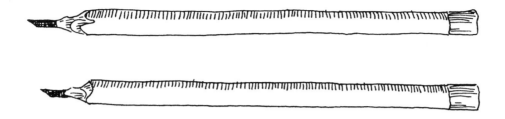

Figure 1-5
Wooden drawing pencils.

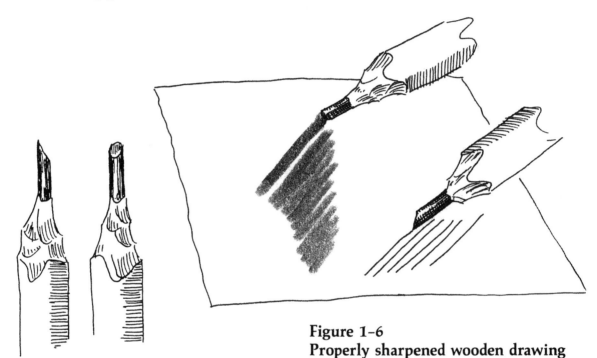

Figure 1-6
Properly sharpened wooden drawing
pencils and the lines the points produce.

Erasers

An eraser is not so much something used to correct mistakes as it is a tool used to achieve effects in pencil drawings. I use a Pink Pearl eraser and a kneaded eraser. The latter, which is a critical requirement for making pencil drawings, consists of material that you knead and mold with your fingers into shapes that are then pressed—not rubbed—on your drawing to selectively lighten a pencil passage or part of one. A kneaded eraser can be pinched to a sharp edge that will lift a sliver of graphite from a dark passage to produce a nice highlight. After each use the dirty part is kneaded into the interior of the eraser so that it will not be inadvertently printed on a clean area of your drawing. Some of the effects obtained by use of the kneaded eraser are shown in figure 1-7.

Figure 1–7
The selective lightening effects of pressing the kneaded eraser on dark pencil passages can be seen on the markings to the left of the cat. This technique was used to show the whiskers as well as the highlights on the ears and around the face.

Paper

For practice and for very casual drawing, bond typing paper is fine, as it will take both ink and pencil lines very well. There are also inexpensive pads of general drawing paper, available in art supply stores, that are usually good for pencil and often for ink drawing as well (but you should be sure that any pads you buy for ink drawing are suitable for it). The coarser pads that are made for pencil or charcoal work may not take a good ink line, because of the porosity of the paper surface, which causes the ink to feather out. An art supply store should be able to help you make a good selection.

The papers described below can also be very helpful in achieving some of the effects that I demonstrate in the lessons in the later chapters.

Vellum-Finish Paper
Vellum-finish paper has a slightly rough finish that provides a "tooth" to which pencil graphite adheres. Ink generally takes quite well also to a vellum finish. I use seventy-pound vellum-finish paper, which is available in office supply stores and print shops, for most of my pencil and pen work.

Bristol Board
Bristol board is a standard heavy drawing paper that is a favorite of artists. It is available in pads and in several weights. I use two-ply kid-finish bristol board. Illustration board, the standard paper used by illustrators, is simply bristol board bonded to a heavy paper to provide a good, sturdy, large piece of paper. Bristol board is usually available in 9" × 12" and 11" × 14" pads, as well as in larger pads.

Tracing Vellum

Tracing vellum, a good-quality drafting paper, is also available in pads. It is translucent and much more sturdy and permanent than tracing paper. It is most useful for preparing your final working drawing for transfer to the paper on which you will complete it. It takes both ink and pencil very well.

Linen-Finish Paper

Linen-finish paper is an inexpensive paper that I sometimes use for pencil drawings. The linen texture is embossed into the surface of the paper and shows up in the dark passages of the final drawing, if you draw carefully. Figure 1-8 shows a drawing done on linen paper.

Coquille Paper

Coquille paper is a heavy paper with a very pronounced pebbly finish. It is frequently used by illustrators for drawings that are printed just as text is, with no need for screening. The high spots on the paper pick up the graphite or crayon and produce a dot pattern. If the implement is pressed more firmly, the graphite or crayon covers more of the paper between the bumps, thus making a darker area. Varying tones are produced this way: not by placing lighter or darker shades on the paper with different-weight pencils but rather by covering more or less of the paper with the uniformly dark "dots."

Fixative

Pencil drawings can be smeared very easily. Fixatives, available at art supply stores, can be sprayed onto your drawing to make the graphite from the pencil adhere to the paper and not rub off so easily. I, however, use plain, clear spray enamel because it works as well and costs much less. A half dozen very light coatings, allowed to dry for a few seconds between applications, work best. If you put the spray on too heavily it will float some of the graphite around on your drawing.

Figure 1-8
A pencil sketch done on linen-finish paper. Note the linen pattern in the dark areas.

2
Copying, Enlarging, Reducing, and Transferring a Subject

Copying a Subject

Choosing Your Picture Size

Transferring a Composition to Final Paper

An important step in drawing is to get a faint, easily erased, correctly proportioned pencil image onto the paper that you intend to use for your final drawing. First, I make a composition drawing on other paper. I work this drawing over, doing all the erasing and adjusting that is necessary to get things just right, and then I transfer the "good" part of that drawing to my final paper. Erasing not only roughs up the paper surface, making it impossible to get decent, sharp pen lines, but also spoils the paper surface for pencil tones because the roughened areas take the graphite differently. It is good practice to treat the surface of your final paper as gently as you can so it is advisable to do a separate composition sketch each time.

This chapter is devoted to showing you how to copy a photograph or a drawing of your subject, reduce it if it is larger than you want your drawing to be, enlarge it if it is too small, and transfer it to your final paper so you can complete it with pen or pencil.

Copying a Subject

Your subject may be a photograph, another drawing, a print or painting, or a live cat in a zoo or in your living room. The living animal is, of course, the best reference, but, unfortunately, the real thing is not always available. Printed material often must be used.

Copying a Reference at the Same Size
There is an easy way to copy printed material by drawing squares on tracing paper (or, better yet, on clear acetate or mylar film, using ink that is made for these surfaces) and placing this grid on top of your reference (see figure 2–1A). Then draw the same-size squares on your composition paper; copy the reference by noting where the lines go in each one of these squares and drawing the same thing in the corresponding square on your paper. You will be surprised how quickly you can copy a complex subject this way. You can then clean up and adjust your drawing to get it just right before you transfer it to your final paper.

Enlarging the Subject
If the squares you draw on your composition paper are the same size as those you are copying from, your drawing will be the same size as the original. If the squares are larger, your resulting drawing will be larger than the original, as shown in figure 2–1B.

Reducing the Subject
To make your drawing smaller than the original, draw the squares smaller than those on the reference (see figure 2–1C).

Choosing Your Picture Size

Most beginners simply start drawing on a piece of paper without regard to how large they want their final drawing to be. You should have a size for your finished product in mind. If, for example, you intend to frame it, then plan to have it an appropriate size for a standard frame. Some standard frame sizes, and the recommended drawing sizes to allow for proper matting, are shown in figure 2–2.

Once you have selected your drawing size, divide the horizontal or vertical edge

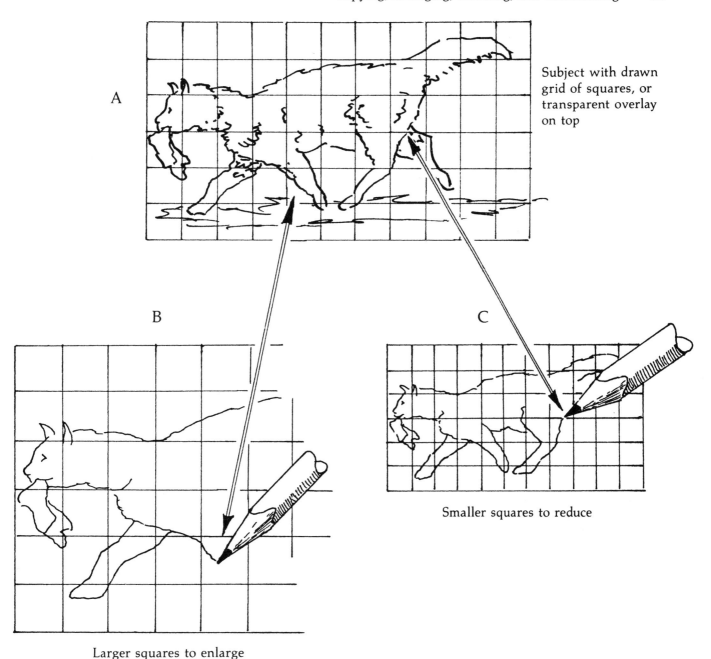

A

Subject with drawn
grid of squares, or
transparent overlay
on top

B

Larger squares to enlarge

C

Smaller squares to reduce

Figure 2-1
To copy or enlarge or reduce a figure,
(A) draw a grid of squares on tracing
paper—or on clear acetate or mylar
film—and place it over the figure you
want to copy. Draw squares of the same
size on your composition paper and,
referring to the grid overlay, draw
similar lines in corresponding squares.

(B) To enlarge the subject, draw larger
squares on your composition paper.
Observe where the outline crosses
various squares on your overlay and
draw similar lines in the corresponding
larger squares. (C) If you want to reduce
the subject, draw smaller squares on
your composition paper and follow the
same procedure.

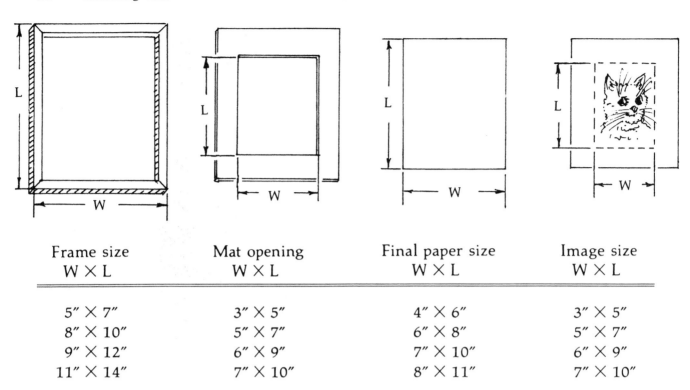

Frame size W × L	Mat opening W × L	Final paper size W × L	Image size W × L
5" × 7"	3" × 5"	4" × 6"	3" × 5"
8" × 10"	5" × 7"	6" × 8"	5" × 7"
9" × 12"	6" × 9"	7" × 10"	6" × 9"
11" × 14"	7" × 10"	8" × 11"	7" × 10"

into the number of divisions necessary to copy your subject in that space. Make squares by using this same dimension to section off the other edge, and then draw in the squares. When your composition drawing is finished, you will be all set to transfer it to your final paper at exactly the correct size.

Figure 2–2
This chart shows the relationship of some standard frame sizes, mats for these sizes, final paper sizes, and the actual image sizes you should draw to fit the frames.

Transferring a Composition to Final Paper

Once your composition drawing is as you want it, you must transfer it to your final paper so that you can complete the pencil or the ink work. To produce a light, easily erased image to work from, blacken the back of your composition drawing with a soft pencil, as shown in figure 2–3A. Place the blackened side down on your final paper, center the image, and trace over the image with a sharp pencil (see figure 2–3B). You will transfer a light image to your final paper, as shown in figure 2–3C. If your drawing will be in

ink, you can lightly erase the pencil lines when you no longer need them to guide your inking. If your drawing will be in pencil, these lines cannot be erased, but they should be light enough so that they do not interfere with your final pencil drawing.

I always work with a sheet of clean paper under my wrist as I draw to keep my wrist clean. That way I avoid smearing any graphite around on the final paper.

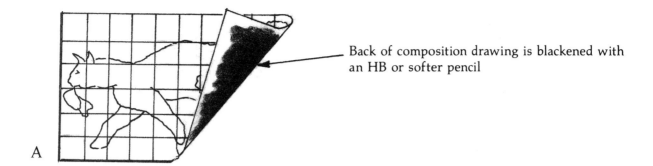

Back of composition drawing is blackened with an HB or softer pencil

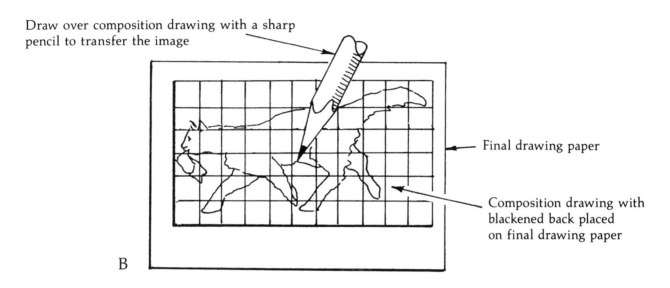

Draw over composition drawing with a sharp pencil to transfer the image

Final drawing paper

Composition drawing with blackened back placed on final drawing paper

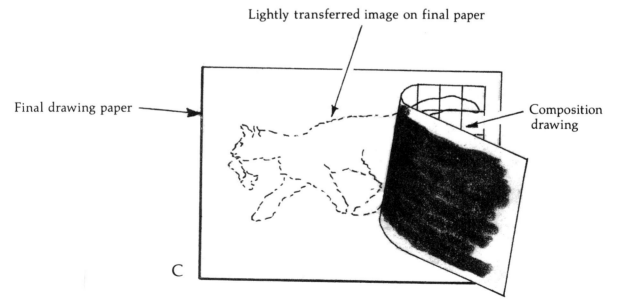

Lightly transferred image on final paper

Final drawing paper

Composition drawing

Figure 2-3
To transfer your composition drawing to your final paper, (A) blacken the back of your composition drawing with a soft pencil. (B) Place the blackened side down on your final paper, and trace over the outline with a sharp pencil. (C) A light image is transferred to your final paper.

3
Pen-and-Ink Techniques

Outlines

Small Line Drawing of a Kitten

Stipple Drawing of a Kitten

Large Line Drawing of a Kitten

Outlines

Ink lines have character and appeal, which go a long way in creating the impression of texture that the viewer perceives in a drawing. Figure 3-1 shows the outline of a kitten done with a smooth line. This outline gives the impression not of a live kitten but of a smooth ceramic statue or an illustration in a child's coloring book. The broken line used in figure 3-2, however, creates the impression of furriness because the line imitates the furry outline of a kitten.

Note that it is not a continuous line—it has pieces missing—yet there is enough there to define the form of the kitten. Additional lines are now necessary to tone the interior of this form to bring out the impression of roundness and texture.

The first three lessons are devoted to showing you how to use different kinds of ink marks to suggest the furry texture of this kitten and also to demonstrating how the considerations vary for drawings of different sizes.

Figure 3-1
Making an outline like this is an improper way to begin a pen sketch of a kitten because the solid outline does not suggest fur.

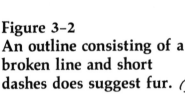

Figure 3-2
An outline consisting of a broken line and short dashes does suggest fur.

LESSON 1
Small Line Drawing of a Kitten

Tools and Materials
Crowquill pen, or any reasonably fine-point ink pen; waterproof India or drawing ink; bond typing paper, or any other paper that takes ink well. (I used my 0 technical pen and seventy-pound vellum-finish paper for these illustrations.)

Procedure
The completed sketch of the kitten, shown in figure 3-3, should be used as a guide as you follow the instructions to complete your drawing of this subject.

Use the composition drawing and grid shown in figure 3-4 to prepare your own working drawing. In this lesson you will

Figure 3-3
In this pen sketch of a kitten, the lines that produce the tone go more or less in the direction of the fur.

A B C D E F G

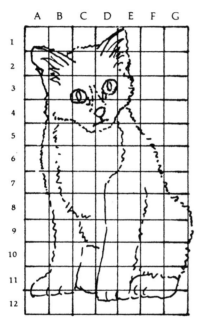

Figure 3-4
The composition drawing for Lessons 1 and 2.

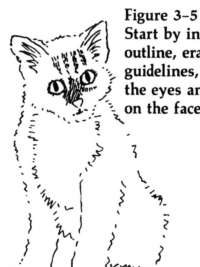

Figure 3-5
Start by inking in the outline, erasing the pencil guidelines, and then doing the eyes and dark features on the face.

make a small drawing, so use one-quarter-inch squares on your grid and follow the instructions in Chapter 2 for preparing and transferring your composition drawing to your final paper.

Use a broken line to ink in the outline of the kitten (figure 3–5), and then erase the pencil guidelines so they will not be smeared all over your drawing as you work. Now follow the instructions in the captions accompanying figures 3–5 through 3–9 to complete your drawing.

Be careful when you hatch over the light part of the eyes. It is easy to over-

do this toning and make them too dark. If you do make this mistake, however, don't worry. Remember, this is a simple drawing and you are learning at this point. The blackened composition drawing you made is good for several transfers, so if this first sketch doesn't satisfy you, just transfer the outline to another piece of paper and try again.

When you do the shadow under the kitten, use horizontal lines. This helps create the impression that the surface is horizontal.

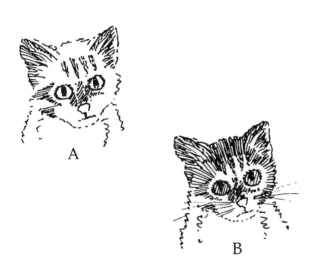

Figure 3-6
(A) Continue with the darker features on the face, and then do the ears. (B) After you have completed the rest of the head, carefully hatch the light parts of the eyes.

Figure 3-7
Indicate the fur texture on the white chest by using just a few lines. Then add the dark stripes on the legs.

Figure 3-8
Hatch the darker fur on the legs, going right over the lines showing the stripes. Then start toning the hip.

Figure 3-9
Finish the hip by using a little crosshatching on the darkest part next to the body. Then complete the undersides and put the shadow in place.

LESSON 2
Stipple Drawing of a Kitten

Ink stipple with a fine pen can create very fine detail. You will see, however, that it takes longer to complete a drawing with stipple than it does with lines because so little ink is placed on the paper with each dot.

When I do a stipple drawing I usually place the darkest features in first, and then I go over the drawing to add the lighter tones. Because it is easy to lose some of the dark markings when you add the lighter tones, build up the dark markings as you go along if you see them disappearing.

Tools and Materials
Crowquill pen, or any reasonably fine-point ink pen; waterproof India or drawing ink; bond typing paper, or any other paper that takes ink well. (I used my 5×0 technical pen and seventy-pound vellum-finish paper for the fine-pen illustration.)

Procedure
Two completed stipple drawings of the kitten are shown in figure 3–10, one made with a relatively coarse-point artist's fountain pen, and the other made with a very fine, 5×0 technical pen. Use these to guide you as you follow the instructions.

Using dots only (no lines), follow the sequence in figures 3–11 through 3–14 to complete your stipple drawing. When you finish, place a few dots outside the outline near the dark areas to eliminate a cutout look—make very few, however, or you will simply extend the cat's body. Check your drawing against figure 3–10.

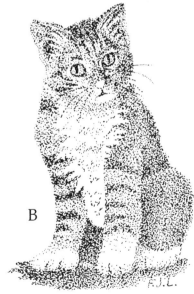

Figure 3–10
In these ink stipple drawings of the kitten, A was done with a coarse-point pen (artist's fountain pen) and B with a very fine pen (5×0 technical pen).

Figure 3-11
Stipple the outline, the fur marks on the white breast, and then the dark markings on the face and chin.

Figure 3-12
Finish the eyes, the ears, and the rest of the head. Then add a few whiskers—all with dots.

Figure 3-13
Stipple the stripes on the legs.

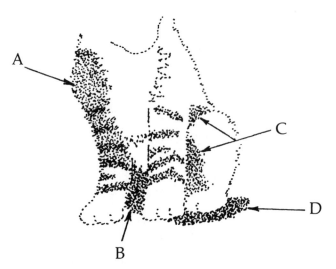

Figure 3-14
Complete the fur tones (referring to A), making sure you don't lose the stripes. Darken the stripes, if necessary, as you go along. Put in the dark underbody (refer to B), and be sure to give the hip some form by darkening it, as shown at C. Stipple the shadow (referring to D).

LESSON 3
Large Line Drawing of a Kitten

Larger drawings require a somewhat different approach from the one you might use for small drawings. More lines are required to cover the paper with ink, and therefore you can indicate more detail. Small drawings, such as those you did in the first two lessons, are more difficult in a sense because so few lines, or dots, are required that each one is very important, and even a few too many can ruin a sketch. Larger drawings, such as this study of the same kitten, can be done with bolder pens, although the finer the pen used, the finer detail you can produce, as illustrated in this lesson.

Tools and Materials
Medium-point pen; bond typing paper, or any other paper that takes ink well. (I used my artist's fountain pen and twenty-pound copier paper for these drawings.)

Procedure
Use figure 3–15 to make your composition drawing for this larger sketch, and then transfer it to your final paper, following the instructions in Chapter 2.

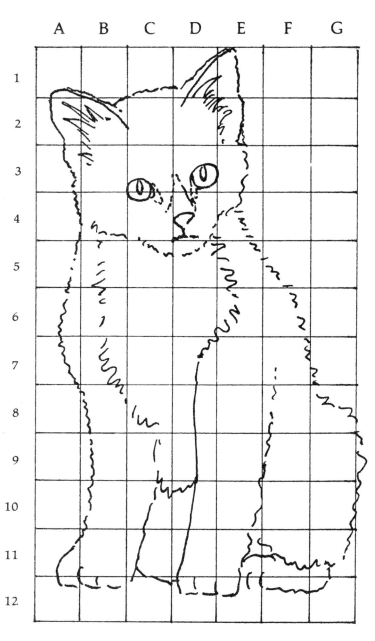

Figure 3–15
This composition drawing for a larger sketch of the kitten has one-half-inch squares.

Figure 3–16
An artist's fountain pen was used to make the completed line drawing of the kitten. The pen has a somewhat broad— or medium—point.

The completed sketch, shown in figure 3–16, was done in a casual, scribble-stroke style that produces a "loose" effect. Note that this kind of stroke enhances the impression of fur.

I used just a little crosshatching in the dark area between the kitten's paws. The rest of the toning was produced with hatch marks only.

Follow the instructions accompanying figures 3–17 through 3–21 to complete your drawing, referring to figure 3–16 as you go along.

When your drawing is at the stage shown in figure 3–21, refer to figure 3–16 and add the dark area between the kitten's paws. Then add the shadow at the bottom.

I did this drawing using a fairly coarse point in my artist's fountain pen. To show you how a fine-point drawing of this same size looks, I did another drawing, figure 3–22, with my 5×0 technical pen, which has a very sharp point. You can do this drawing yourself with a fine point by following the same steps that you have already followed, but this time use figure 3–22 as a guide. The finer point allows much sharper development of details.

Figure 3-18
Hatch the ears but let the long, lighter hairs remain evident. Add some tone under the chin.

Figure 3-17
Use a broken line and short hatch marks to ink in the outline. Then erase the pencil guidelines and start the eyes and facial area by putting the darkest marks in place.

Figure 3-19
Finish hatching the head, leaving some light patches. Add the whiskers—just a few. Then carefully hatch across the eyes to tone them a little.

Figure 3–20
Put the darker markings in place on the legs.

Figure 3–21
Complete the hatching of each part of the kitten, one part at a time, going right over the dark markings. Space the hatch marks farther apart on the very light areas, such as the kitten's lower left leg and paws.

Figure 3–22
A 5×0 technical pen was used for this drawing. Its very fine point can create much finer detail at this scale than can the artist's fountain pen with its coarser point.

4
Pencil Techniques

Lines and Tones

Pencil Drawing of a Black-and-White Kitten

Small Drawing Done with a Sharp Pencil

*Small Drawing Using Broad-Point and
  Sharp Pencils*

Lines and Tones

Drawing pencils come in various degrees of hardness. The harder a pencil, the lighter a mark it will make on the paper. The designations of hardness of leads or pencils go from 6H, a very hard lead, through progressively softer leads, 4H, 2H, H, HB, B, 2B, 3B, and 4B, to 6B, a very soft lead. The various brands differ in hardness for the same designation; that is, an HB pencil of one brand may be softer (darker) or harder (lighter) than an HB of another brand. If you are getting several pencils to use with the lessons in this book, I recommend that you get

HB 0.5mm mechanical pencil

HB wooden pencil

HB drafting lead in lead holder

B drafting lead in lead holder

B 0.5mm mechanical pencil

3B drafting lead in lead holder

4B wooden pencil

6B wooden pencil

Figure 4–1
The range of lines and tones produced by my drawing pencils on seventy-pound vellum-finish paper. You should make a similar reference chart using your pencils and a piece of the paper type you will be using for most of your drawings.

them all from the same maker. In any event, it is a good idea to make a reference chart similar to the one in figure 4–1 so that you can see at any time the relative difference in darkness of the lines and broad tones made by your various pencils when they are used on the paper you work with most frequently. This way, even if you have pencils from different makers, you will be able to see how dark or how light a mark they make. This can become quite important as you work through a pencil drawing.

The next several lessons will acquaint you with some of the techniques of pencil drawing. As with pen and ink, whether you are doing small or large drawings makes a difference. Larger ones allow you to create more detail and to use broad points to tone the larger areas quickly and smoothly. Sharper points allow the depiction of finer detail than broader points and, therefore, are more frequently used on smaller drawings in which there is seldom room to place much detail— every stroke must count. Wooden drawing pencils are normally sharpened to provide both broad and sharp points at the same time (see figure 1–6). Drafting leads can be sharpened the same way.

LESSON 4
Pencil Drawing of a Black-and-White Kitten

Tools and Materials
HB, B, and 4B pencils; seventy-pound vellum-finish paper; kneaded eraser.

Procedure
The completed pencil drawing of a black-and-white kitten, shown in figure 4–2, will give you an idea of how to treat dark as well as light fur and how to get that impression of fur you will want in most of your cat drawings.

The composition drawing, which you should draw or copy and transfer to your final paper according to the instructions in Chapter 2, is shown in figure 4–3. I used one-half-inch squares for this drawing.

**Figure 4–2
The completed pencil drawing of a kitten in a flowerpot. Use this figure to guide your work as you follow the step-by-step instructions.**

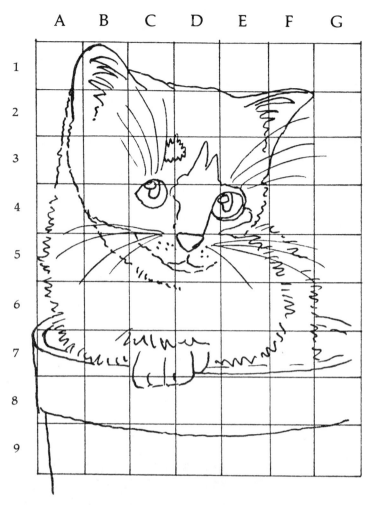

Figure 4-3
In the composition drawing for Lesson 4 I used one-half-inch squares.

Studying figures 4-4 and 4-5 and reading the captions will give you a general idea of how to make a drawing like this. Your pencil outlines should be light at all times, especially where the subject is light, as in figure 4-4. In this case, a 4B pencil is appropriate for doing the eyelid outlines (at B), although an HB would be more appropriate if the kitten's face were light rather than dark. Since this kitten's mouth and neck are light, an HB pencil is used to indicate the cheeks, lower jaw, and nose (at C), and the light inner surfaces of the ears (at D). Where the black fur forms the kitten's outline, such as on the top of the head, a 4B pencil is a good choice to form the furlike outline, as at E.

Read the considerations shown under figure 4-5 and check the illustration to see how they are applied. Then start your drawing of this subject on your final paper. Constantly refer to figure 4-2 as you do your drawing to insure that your tones are developing properly.

Complete the kitten's eyes and face, as shown in figure 4-6. Be careful not to lose the little highlights in each eye that make the eyes glisten. (If you do lose the highlights, you can always put a little dab of white paint on the eyes when your drawing is finished.)

I used my kneaded eraser in several places as I drew this kitten. First I suggested some eyelashes and whiskers over the dark fur, as you see at A in figure 4-7. I did this by pinching the kneaded eraser to a sharp edge and then touching this edge to the dark area. Doing this several times produced each

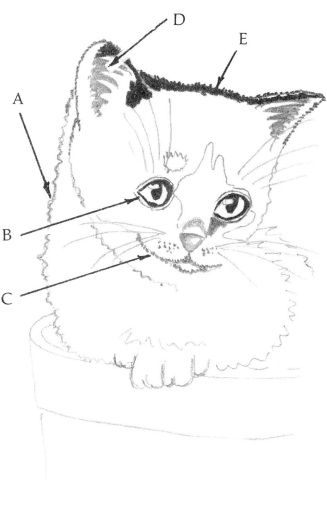

Figure 4–4
General considerations: (A) Keep the outline light, especially where the fur is light. (B) Use a sharp 4B pencil for the eyes, leaving the little highlight in each eye. (C) Use an HB pencil to indicate the lips and the jaw and (D) the inner ears. (E) Use a 4B pencil for the dark fur.

Figure 4–5
General considerations: (A) Outline the dark fur areas by making irregular marks and dashes with the 4B pencil. (B) Then fill in these dark areas with the 4B pencil. (C) Fill in the dark areas with marks like this. (D) Leave a little irregularity in the darks to suggest highlights on the fur. (E) Use an HB pencil to tone the light fur outlines and light patches of fur. (F) Use a sharp HB pencil to put a few fur marks on the lightly toned areas.

A   B   C

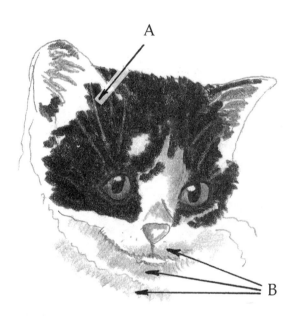

Figure 4–6
To complete the eyes, (A) use a 4B pencil to darken the irises and to outline the eyelids. Be sure to leave the little white highlights untouched. (B) Draw the dark fur with your 4B pencil. (C) Darken the eyes with a broad-point HB pencil but leave the highlights alone. Use a B pencil to darken the white ring around the eyes.

Figure 4–7
(A) Add eyelashes and whiskers over the dark areas by pinching the kneaded eraser to a sharp edge and touching that edge to the drawing. (B) Use a broad-point HB pencil to suggest shadows in the light fur areas.

eyelash or whisker. Each time I did it, however, I folded the dirty part of the eraser into the middle of the lump and produced a new surface that I then pinched to an edge. I also used the eraser on the kitten's ears because they were too dark after I first toned them. One or two pressings (no rubbing) of the kneaded eraser lifted the proper amount of graphite from the drawing.

When you complete the dark parts of

the kitten's fur, switch to harder pencils to do the toning and details in the white fur, as you see at B in figure 4–7. Use the broad point to tone the shadows and the sharp point to put in the lines that help suggest fur.

I used my broad-point HB pencil to tone the flowerpot, which was left light because I didn't want it to stand out and detract from the kitten.

LESSON 5
Small Drawing Done with a Sharp Pencil

Tools and Materials
Sharp B pencil (I used a 0.5 millimeter mechanical pencil with a B lead); seventy-pound vellum-finish paper; kneaded eraser.

Procedure
Copy figure 4–8 and transfer it, as described in Chapter 2, to your final paper. I used one-quarter-inch squares for this and the following lesson. The drawing you will use as a reference for this lesson is shown in figure 4–9.

Be sure to use a B lead because anything harder, such as an HB, will not let you get the dark fur dark enough. By rubbing the B lead gently on the paper, you will be able to get the light shades also. If any of it turns out too dark, just press your kneaded eraser to the area to lighten it.

Do the light fur, the nose and mouth area, and the insides of the ears with a light touch of the pencil. Let most of the strokes show because, at this scale, they form not only the primary fur indication but also the gray toning that indicates the shades and shadows in the light fur. Refer to figure 4–9 as you complete these parts of the drawing.

The dark fur areas are done with firm pressure of the B lead to get the darker tone. Figure 4–10 at A shows how to fill in the dark fur with a sort of scribble stroke in the direction that the fur lies on the animal. Leave white paper between the clusters of lines. The next step, indicated at B, is to go over the dark areas to remove the white paper. Use the same pencil but with less pressure so that the earlier marks still show through to suggest the fur.

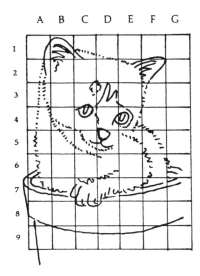

Figure 4–8
I used one-quarter-inch squares in this smaller composition drawing of the kitten and flowerpot.

Figure 4–9
A drawing done using only a sharp B pencil. The pencil was pressed heavily in drawing the darks and pressed lightly to get the lighter tones.

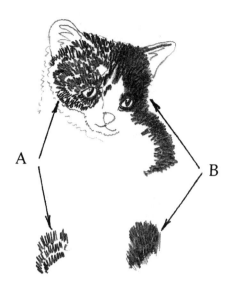

Figure 4-10
(A) Make marks like this in the dark areas by using a sharp B pencil. (B) Then, using the same pencil, go over the whole dark area a little less heavily to cover all of the white patches left in the darks. Be sure to let the initial pencil strokes show through.

The eyes are a little difficult to complete at this small size. Figure 4-11 shows, in enlarged drawings, what you should do to leave the little highlight in each eye. If you find it very difficult to keep the highlights from disappearing, complete your drawing and add a tiny touch of white paint when you are finished. If you do this, use a good, sharply pointed brush.

The flowerpot is toned with light strokes of the same B point (see figure 4-9).

Figure 4-11
(A) The eyes appear like this in your working drawing. (B) Darken the pupils with a sharp B pencil, but leave the white highlights alone. (C) Very lightly tone the rest of each eyeball, but don't touch the highlight. This toning should be done as your last step in completing the drawing.

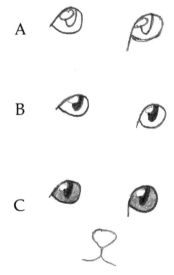

LESSON 6
Small Drawing Using Broad-Point and Sharp Pencils

Tools and Materials
Sharp and broad-point HB and B pencils; seventy-pound vellum-finish paper; kneaded eraser.

Procedure
In figure 4–12, another drawing of the same kitten subject as in the previous lesson, both broad-point and sharp pencils were used to do the toning.

To do your drawing, transfer to your final paper another outline of the subject from the transfer sheet you made for Lesson 5. Refer to figures 4–13 through 4–15 for step-by-step instructions. After completing the kitten part of the drawing, use a sharp HB pencil to trim up the edges of the flowerpot and to add some whiskers. You cannot, in a drawing of this size, use the kneaded eraser to help show the eyelashes and whiskers as you did in the much larger drawing in Lesson 4.

Figure 4–12
Another small pencil drawing of the kitten. At this scale all you can do with the broad-point pencils is to place a few major tone areas where they belong. Use a few strokes with the sharp pencils to clean up some edges and make some fur marks in the lightly toned places.

Figure 4–13
Use a broad-point HB pencil for the gray tones and a sharp B pencil for the eyes.

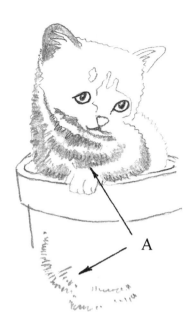

Figure 4–14
Use a sharp HB pencil to suggest fur by making marks, similar to those at A, directly over the gray tones.

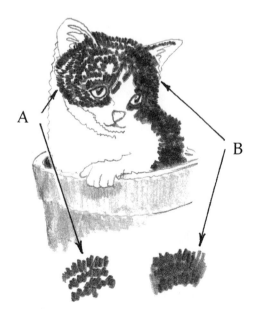

Figure 4–15
Use a broad-point B pencil to start the dark tones, as at A, with some white paper showing between them. Then go over the whole area, as at B, to fill in the white spaces. Use a broad-point HB pencil for the flowerpot toning.

5
Finding and Using Reference Materials

You cannot draw well those things that you cannot see and do not know unless you have good photographs, drawings, or paintings as references. The real thing is the best reference for anything we draw, but it is not always possible, or practical, to go to the woods, jungle, zoo, or museum when we want to draw a particular kind of animal. Even if, for example, you own a cat, it may not cooperate and pose as you would like when you want to draw it. In that case a photograph may have to suffice. Good reference materials are absolutely essential to good animal drawing.

If you are going to draw a tiger, you should first get as many photographs of tigers as you can. Study them. Observe the proportions of the tiger's head and legs to its body; note that the tiger is a very muscular animal with a big and heavy frame; see that it has a prominent furry chin, whiskered cheeks, and a relatively large nose. Only then do a drawing from a photograph, as I did in figure 5-1. By following this advice you will gain some understanding of the relationship of the parts of your subject and will produce a more realistic drawing than if you simply try to duplicate what one photograph shows.

Good drawing is mostly observation, and you must have something representative to observe. The cheetah has a smaller head, in relation to its body, than the tiger (see figure 5-2). So if you took the outline of a cheetah and put stripes on it,

as I did in figure 5-3, you wouldn't have a very convincing tiger. Good reference photographs are really so easy to come by that, until you know the anatomy of your subject really well from drawing it many times, you should make use of them. The next chapter shows you how to learn something about the structure of animals from their photographs so that you can begin to create poses for which you have no reference.

Learning something about your subject is especially necessary if you intend to create a pose that you don't happen to find in any references. Then you must understand even more about how the subject is constructed. I will go into this aspect of learning from reference photographs in the next chapter.

Your local library is perhaps the best source of reference material. For the subject of cats, both domestic and wild, first look in the subject card catalog under the headings Cats, Lions, Tigers, Animals, and African Animals. You will find many books listed that have photographs large enough to show the kind of detail you will need to do a convincing drawing. Sometimes the photograph of a particular pose you like will not show necessary detail, often because of shadows. That is when other photographs are required so that you can see what the details look like in that shadowy area and incorporate that knowledge as you draw.

Figure 5-1
A tiger has a large head in proportion to its powerful body.

Figure 5-2
A cheetah has a relatively small head in proportion to its body.

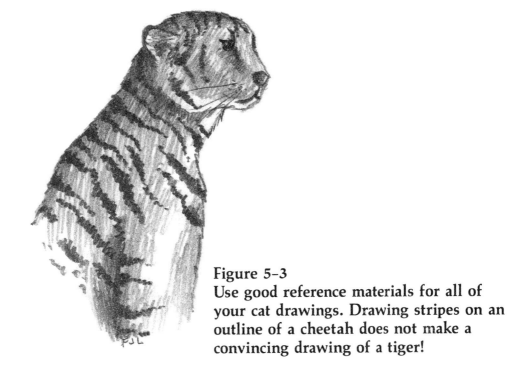

Figure 5-3
Use good reference materials for all of your cat drawings. Drawing stripes on an outline of a cheetah does not make a convincing drawing of a tiger!

6
The Basic Structure of Cats

A Geometric Approach

Other Features

A Geometric Approach

Before drawing animals, fish, flowers, or birds, I always try to see what the underlying geometry of the subject is. This lets me make small variations in my drawing with some confidence that what I do will actually be representative of the subject. I do not mean that the geometric approach I explain in this chapter—the one that I use as a drawing aid—has anything to do with cat physiology or structure. It does not. All it does is allow me to sketch more quickly a reasonably good cat outline, regardless of whether or not I have any reference photograph that has the particular pose I want to draw. I use photographs of my subject to establish certain proportions, and then I use these proportions when I am making variations in poses of the subject.

This approach is covered in considerable detail for birds, animals, and flowers in my book, *Wildlife Sketching*. (See the listing Other Books by Frank J. Lohan at the end of this book.)

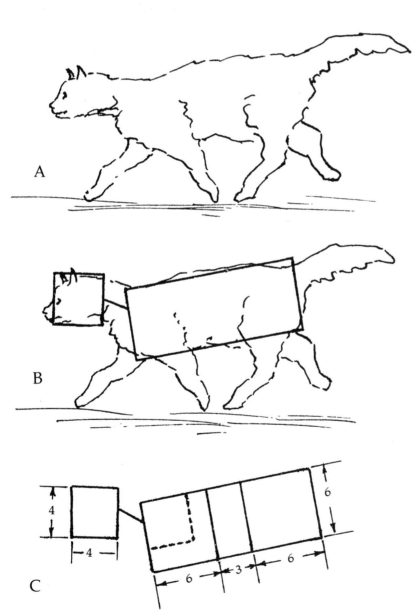

Figure 6-1
To determine the geometry of a cat profile, (A) trace the outline from a photograph. (B) Draw a square to encompass the cat's head and a rectangle to encompass its body. (C) Determine how many squares make up the body and what the proportions of the squares and rectangles are. The numbers simply represent relative proportions: three is half of six, etc.

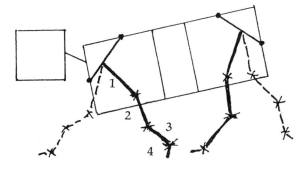

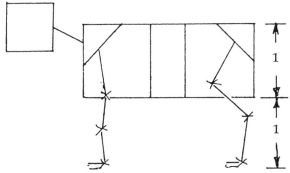

Figure 6–2
Place the legs on the drawing. Give each leg four segments, and attach them to the middle of the diagonal lines at the front and back of the body rectangle.

Figure 6–3
The legs are straightened out here so that the structure represents a standing cat. This figure now relates the height of the cat's body to its thickness.

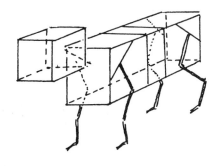

Figure 6–4
The proportions of figures 6–2 and 6–3 are used to sketch a three-quarter view of the standing cat.

House Cats

I traced the profile of a house cat (figure 6–1A) from a photograph. I then drew a square and a rectangle on the sketch to block in the cat's head and body, as you see in figure 6–1B. I next determined how many squares made up the body rectangle and what the proportions are of the head square to the basic body square (figure 6–1C). The numbers are simply to show the proportions of each square: six is twice as long as three, etc.

You can see from figure 6–1C that the body is two-and-a-half squares long and that the square that outlines the cat's head is about two-thirds of the dimensions of a basic body square.

The next thing I determined from the tracing of the cat was the relationship of the legs to the body. This relationship can be estimated by using four lines—1, 2, 3, and 4 in figure 6–2—attached to the cat structure on the short diagonals shown in

the figure. This is not to imply that the cat's bone structure is at all like what I show. These lines simply represent apparent relationships based on the external appearance of the cat.

Figure 6–3 shows how I use these relationships to alter a pose. Here I made the cat stand upright rather than trot, as it was doing in the photograph I initially used. This framework shows that the cat's body is about as high off the ground as it is thick.

I used the proportions so far established to draw a three-quarter-view framework of the standing cat (figure 6–4). You can use these same proportions to draw a framework of the cat in any position, just as long as you keep the perspective correct. You can make these composition sketches freehand, and very quickly you will be able to establish difference poses.

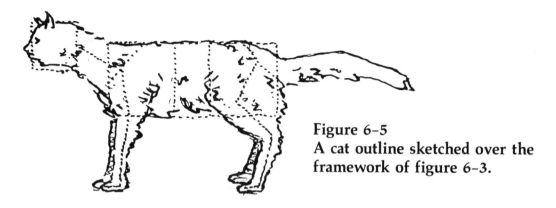

Figure 6-5
A cat outline sketched over the framework of figure 6-3.

Figure 6-6
A cat outline sketched over the framework of figure 6-4.

Figure 6-7
Two more cat outlines, each based on quick framework sketches of the body proportions developed in figures 6-1, 6-2, and 6-3.

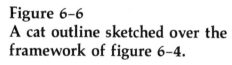

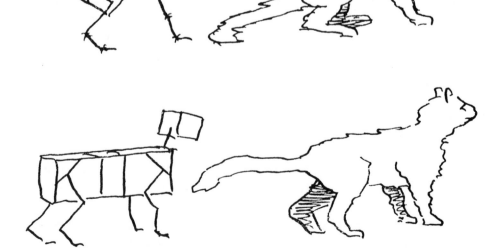

The purpose of these framework sketches is demonstrated in figures 6–5 and 6–6, in which I have sketched cat outlines over the frameworks of the last two figures. I make the framework sketches on any paper and then place tracing paper—or tracing vellum—over the framework. I draw the cat outline on the tracing paper, blacken the back of the tracing paper, and then transfer the outline to my final paper—all explained in Chapter 2. Two additional poses, based on first doing framework sketches and then stretching cat outlines over them, are shown in figure 6–7. I recommend that you try a few of these simple exercises to prove to yourself that you can do them fairly readily and produce a reasonably realistic cat outline. Use the proportions shown in figures 6–1 and 6–2 to make your drawings.

Other Cats

The procedures we have just explored to determine the proportions of a house cat can be applied to other cats (and, of course, to other animals). Figures 6–8 and 6–9 show outlines of a cheetah and a tiger that I traced from photographs. The frameworks and proportions I determined from these outlines are shown in figures 6–10 and 6–11. You can see that the differences between these proportions and those of a house cat, reproduced in figure 6–12 for comparison, are small. But taking the differences into account is very important if your drawings are to be realistic. The cat's body, for instance, is two-and-a-half squares long, the tiger's is two-and-three-quarters squares long, and the cheetah's is two-and-one-third squares long. The heads likewise differ slightly; the cat's is two-thirds of a body

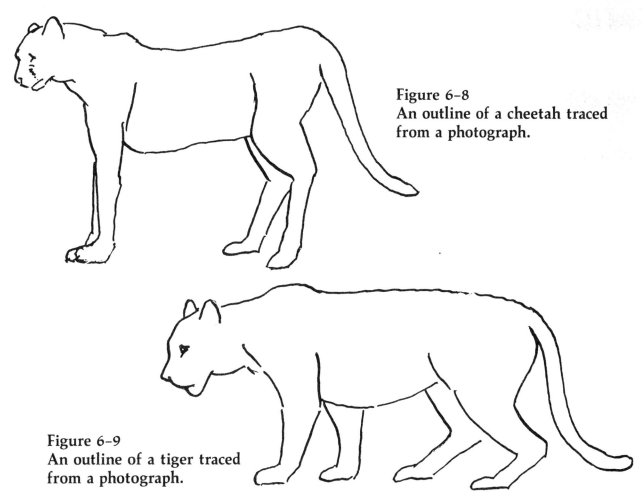

**Figure 6–8
An outline of a cheetah traced from a photograph.**

**Figure 6–9
An outline of a tiger traced from a photograph.**

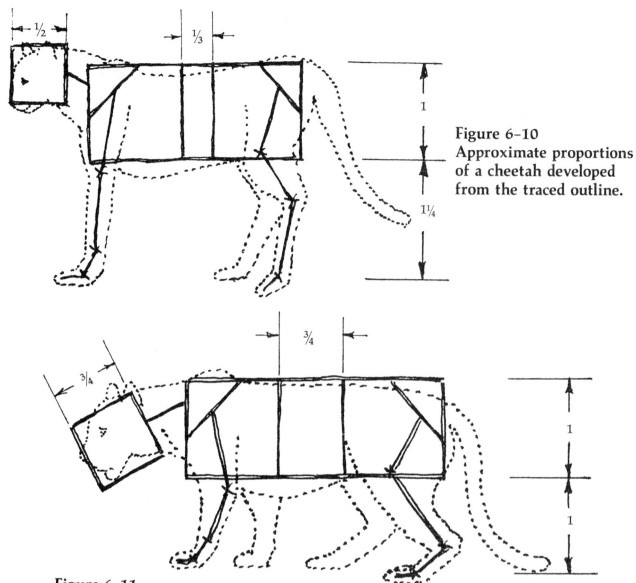

½   ⅓   1   1¼

Figure 6-10
Approximate proportions
of a cheetah developed
from the traced outline.

¾   ¾   1   1

Figure 6-11
Approximate proportions of a tiger developed from the traced outline.

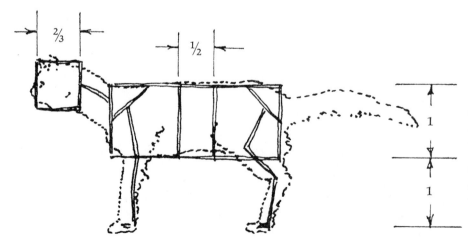

⅔   ½   1   1

Figure 6-12
Approximate proportions
of a house cat for
comparison with those of
the cheetah and the tiger.
These were also
developed from a traced
outline.

square, the tiger's is larger in proportion at three-quarters of a body square, and the cheetah's is smaller in proportion at one-half of a body square. Both the cat and the tiger stand just as high off the ground as their bodies are thick, but the cheetah has longer legs in proportion to its body. It stands one-and-one-quarter body thicknesses high.

Other Features

Obtaining a reasonable outline of your cat is only part of the drawing problem. It is more difficult to get the facial features properly done, for instance, and to do that you need good photographic references. When a cat growls, snarls, or roars (if it is one of the larger cats), the facial muscles wrinkle up to different degrees, and the wrinkles show quite prominently on the sides of the nose. Figure 6–13 is an example of a tiger in a full snarl. The relationship of the snarling

Figure 6–13
A pen drawing, based on a photograph, of a tiger in full snarl.

facial features to a circle is shown in figure 6-14. This sketch was done by tracing the photograph of a snarling tiger's face and drawing over it to determine what geometric relationships I could discover. For comparison, a nonsnarling tiger's face is developed from this sketch in figure 6-15, and the relationship of the features to a circle is shown in figure 6-16. You can see that to convert the snarling tiger to a calm one all I did was raise the lower jaw, drop the upper lip, and remove the wrinkles from the face between the eyes and the nose.

It is not always practical to try to develop a mechanical approach to drawing something as complicated as varying facial features, so good photographic

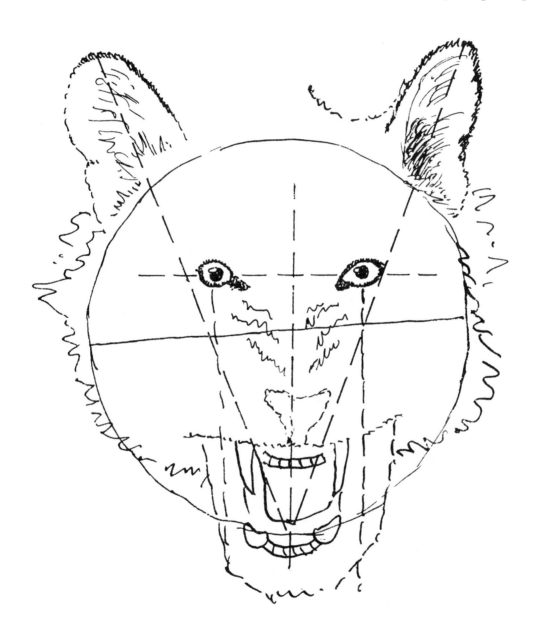

Figure 6-14
A simple geometric analysis of the snarling tiger's face. The features are all related to a circle.

Figure 6–15
A pen drawing of a calm tiger's face.
This was developed from the geometry
of figure 6–16, which was itself based on
that of figure 6–14. When you have
determined geometric relationships, you
can begin to experiment with
composition and have some confidence
that your result will be reasonably
accurate.

references usually are absolutely
necessary to complete the faces of your
cats. Don't miss out, however, on the fun
of trying to find the geometric
relationships of faces. You can sometimes
use what you learn to make minor
changes in a subject, just as I changed a
snarling beast into a calm one.

Figure 6–16
The geometry of the calm tiger's face.

7
Drawing Domestic Cats

Using Photographs

Pencil Drawing of a Siamese Cat

Pen Drawing of a Siamese Cat

Pen Drawing of a White Persian Cat

Pen Drawing of a Short-Haired White Cat

Pencil Drawing of a White Persian Cat

Pencil Drawing of a Short-Haired White Cat

Drawing Different Cats from One Model

Pencil Drawing of a Tortoiseshell-Colored Cat

Pencil Drawing of a Striped Cat

Pencil Drawing of a Black Cat

Pen Drawing of a Striped Kitten

Using Photographs

Probably the most frequently used references for your cat drawings will be photographs. You will have to be very careful when you refer to them, however, because photographs often have severe distortions that are not immediately apparent. We all have grown up looking at newspaper and magazine photographs and at those that we and our friends have taken with our own cameras. Unconsciously, we have come to accept and mentally compensate for many of the distortions. If a close-up photograph is taken, some parts of the subject might be two or three times closer to the lens than other parts, which makes the closer parts appear abnormally large on the finished print. We have all seen this effect, for instance, in photographs of people sitting down with their legs crossed, showing what appear to be huge knees.

Figure 7-1 is a pencil drawing of a cat drawn to look almost exactly like the photographic reference. The nose was the

Figure 7-1
In this drawing of a Siamese cat, made directly from a photograph, the head appears abnormally large because the camera was too close to the subject's head when the photograph was taken. The camera did not compensate for the distortion, which is called foreshortening.

Figure 7-2
(A) In this case the camera is too close to the subject—the cat's back is almost three times as far from the lens as is its head. This will make the head appear abnormally large in the finished print.

(B) Here the cat's back is only about one-and-one-half times as far from the lens as is its head. The resulting foreshortening distortion will hardly be noticeable.

closest thing to the camera, with the rest of the head next closest. The facial features appear unnaturally large in the drawing because the foreshortening is exaggerated. Figure 7-2A shows how such a portrait is recorded by the camera, with the back parts of the cat about three times as far from the lens as the face. In figure 7-2B, the back parts of the cat are only about one-and-one-half times as far from the lens as is the face. When the photographer, using a normal lens, stands at this distance from the cat, the foreshortening distortion will be minor and probably not even noticeable.

Figure 7-3 shows the comparison between what the photograph showed as the outline of the cat's head (dotted lines) and what I did to compensate for the foreshortening distortion (solid lines). My compensation was purely arbitrary—I simply wanted to make the face a little smaller. I then used these adjustments to redraw the same cat, with the result shown in figure 7-4.

Figure 7-3
The dotted lines show the cat's head as it appeared in the photograph. The solid lines show the adjustment I made to get the cat's head in a more correct proportion to its body.

Figure 7–4
I redrew the cat, using the adjusted head proportions, with this result. Use this figure as a guide for your drawing of this subject in Lesson 7.

LESSON 7
Pencil Drawing of a Siamese Cat

Tools and Materials
Broad-point B and broad-point HB pencils; seventy-pound vellum-finish paper; kneaded eraser.

Procedure
Copy figure 7–5 to your working paper, following the instructions in Chapter 2.

Use a B pencil, sharpened as shown in Chapter 1, figure 1–6, so that you have both a broad point and a sharp point, and

follow the instructions accompanying figure 7–6. As you work on your drawing, refer frequently to figure 7–4, the completed pencil drawing, to guide your work. Keep a kneaded eraser handy in case some of your secondary darks get too dark—a touch of the eraser will lighten them quickly. Remember, just press the kneaded eraser to your drawing to remove some of the excess graphite— don't rub it back and forth.

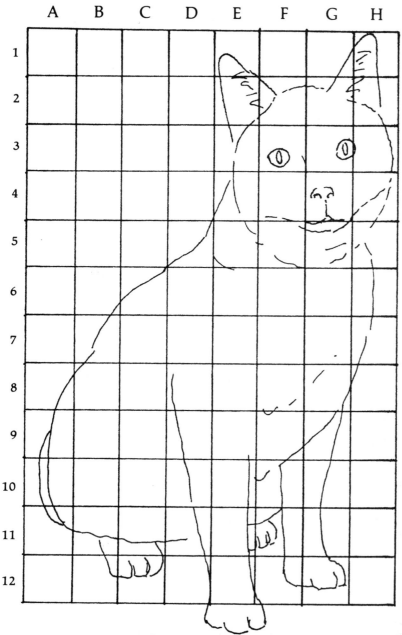

Figure 7–5
This is the gridded outline for your drawings in Lessons 7 and 8.

Figure 7–6
To complete the cat's face, (A) first use a B pencil to heavily outline the eyes, draw the irises, and indicate the other dark areas of the face and ears. (B) Next use the same B pencil to put in the secondary darks. Do not make them so dark that the very dark patches blend in and disappear. Leave the eyeballs and nose white until you have completed the entire head. (C) Finally, tone the eyeballs and nose with a broad-point HB pencil, add a few whiskers, and put a highlight dot on each eye with typewriter correction fluid, which I used in this case, or with white gouache paint.

A   B

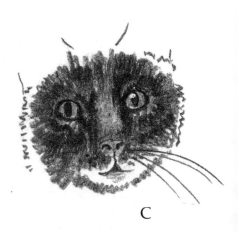

C

LESSON 8
Pen Drawing of a Siamese Cat

Tools and Materials

Fine-point pen (I used my 3×0 technical pen); seventy-pound smooth or vellum-finish paper.

Procedure

Copy and transfer figure 7-5 to your working paper. (If you already have a copy from doing the previous lesson, you can simply trace over the copy you made. One blackened transfer sheet will give you several copies before you have to blacken the back again).

Use figure 7-7, the completed pen drawing, as a guide when you follow the step-by-step instructions accompanying figures 7-8 and 7-9.

To make the legs dark enough may required more than three layers of crosshatching if you do not put the lines very close together.

Erase all pencil guidelines from your drawing when the ink is dry.

Figure 7-7
A pen drawing of the same cat. Use this figure to guide you as you do your drawing of this subject.

Figure 7-8
To complete the cat's face, (A) hatch the outline with short marks and hatch the dark areas on the face and the ears. (B) Crosshatch the ears. (C) Hatch the face again, but run the new lines right over the original ones so that they become darker. (D) Add a few hatch lines to eliminate the patchwork effect of C. Lightly hatch the eyeballs, but leave the little highlights alone. Finally, add a few whiskers.

Figure 7-9
To complete the legs, (A) hatch the dark part of the legs. (B) Crosshatch the same areas with lines at right angles to the first ones. (C) Crosshatch again with a third layer that goes in a different direction from the first two layers.

LESSON 9
Pen Drawing of a White Persian Cat

Tools and Materials
Fine-point pen (I used my 3×0 technical pen); seventy-pound vellum-finish or smooth paper.

Procedure
Drawing white cats is both easy and difficult—easy because it doesn't take much ink to represent the white fur and hard because every mark you put on the

Figure 7-10
A pen drawing of a white Persian cat.

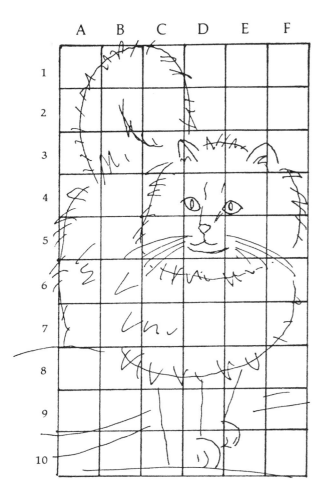

Figure 7-11
The gridded composition outline of the white Persian cat.

paper must be significant. Figure 7-10 shows a simple pen drawing of a Persian cat. You can do this drawing yourself by copying and transferring figure 7-11 to your working paper. It's obvious that very few lines in addition to those that you transfer are required to complete the drawing.

The main thing to remember when you draw long-haired cats is to indicate the clumps of long fur with few lines. There are no actual outlines on figure 7-10 except for the eyes and the legs. All other outlines are suggested by the relatively long fur marks. When your inking is complete and dry, carefully erase the pencil guidelines that are left from your transferred outline.

LESSON 10
Pen Drawing of a Short-Haired White Cat

Tools and Materials
Fine-point pen (I used my 3×0 technical pen); seventy-pound smooth or vellum-finish paper; kneaded eraser.

Procedure
A short-haired white cat is represented by short pen strokes to suggest the short fur. Use figure 7–12 as a guide to make your own quick study of this subject by copying and transferring figure 7–13 to your working paper. Small dashes and a few broken lines are all you need for the outline, and a few suggestions of fur take care of the body texture. Erase the pencil guidelines that remain from your transferred drawing.

Figure 7–12
A pen drawing of a short-haired white cat.

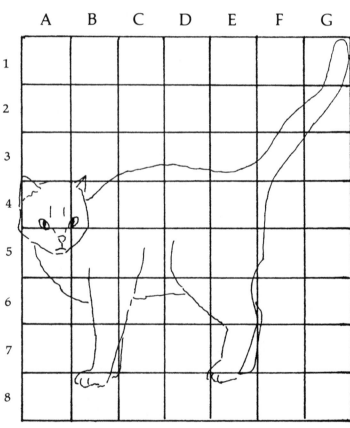

Figure 7–13
The gridded composition outline of the short-haired white cat.

LESSON 11
Pencil Drawing of a White Persian Cat

Tools and Materials
Broad-point B pencil, sharpened as in figure 1-6; seventy-pound vellum-finish paper; kneaded eraser.

Procedure
Make a transfer of figure 7-11 to your working paper, and use figure 7-14 as a guide when you do the pencil drawing. By using the broad point of the pencil

lightly you can do some texturing and shading that were not practical at this scale with the pen. Note that the eyeballs are lightly toned and that a small spot of white gouache paint was placed in each eye to show the glistening highlights.

If any of your texturing gets a little too dark, just press your kneaded eraser to the place to lighten it.

Figure 7–14
A pencil drawing of the white Persian cat.

LESSON 12
Pencil Drawing of a Short-Haired White Cat

Tools and Materials
Broad-point B pencil, sharpened as in figure 1–6; seventy-pound vellum-finish paper; kneaded eraser.

Procedure
Transfer a copy of figure 7–13 to your paper and use figure 7–15, a completed drawing of the cat, to guide your work. There is really little to show in step-by-step instructions since the suggestion of the white cat requires so few marks on the paper. Should any of your marks get too dark, just press your kneaded eraser to the area to lighten it.

Figure 7–15
A pencil drawing of the short-haired white cat.

Drawing Different Cats from One Model

The next few lessons deal with using one pose, or model, to draw differently patterned cats. If you want to draw your own cat, for instance, but want to use a particular pose that you found in a photograph of a different cat, you can get the cat outline from your reference and then sketch the pattern or colors of your cat on it. The cat outline of figure 7–13 will be used here in drawing several differently colored cats.

LESSON 13
Pencil Drawing of a Tortoiseshell-Colored Cat

Tools and Materials
Both sharp and broad-point B pencils;
seventy-pound vellum-finish paper;
kneaded eraser.

Procedure
Figure 7–16 shows the finished pencil
drawing; use it as a guide as you follow
the instructions.

Transfer the outline of figure 7–13 to
your paper and lightly draw the dark
pattern areas on the outline, referring to
figure 7–16. Then follow the suggestions
in figure 7–17 to complete your drawing
of a tortoiseshell-colored cat. Remember
to keep the toning in the white fur areas
very light. You may want to switch to a
broad-point HB pencil to do these light
areas if you cannot get the B pencil to
make light enough marks.

Probably the most troublesome part of
these small drawings will be the little
white highlights on the eyes. It is not
easy to get a tiny dot of white paint just
where you want it. Practice a little on
separate pieces of paper on which you
have drawn just eyes at about the size
you see in this book. Sometimes I use the
end of a piece of pencil lead from my 0.5-
millimeter pencil, which I dip into the
gouache and then print on the eyeball.
Other times I use a number 1 watercolor
brush very carefully, after making a few
practice dots on another sheet.

Figure 7–16
**A pencil drawing of a tortoiseshell-
colored cat.**

Figure 7–17
**To complete your drawing of the
tortoiseshell-colored cat, (A) darken the
eyes and all the other black markings
with a B pencil. (B) Use the same pencil,
but lightly this time, to complete the
medium tones, the shading on the white
fur, and the eyeballs. A dot of white
gouache paint completes the eye
highlights, and strokes with a sharp B
pencil add the whiskers.**

A

B

LESSON 14
Pencil Drawing of a Striped Cat

Tools and Materials
Sharp and broad-point B pencils; seventy-pound vellum-finish paper; kneaded eraser.

Procedure
The finished drawing of the striped cat, shown in figure 7–18, should be your reference as you complete your drawing of this subject by following the instructions accompanying figure 7–19.

First transfer a copy of figure 7–13 to your paper and lightly indicate on it where the stripes fall (see figure 7–19A).

Next put the dark stripes in place with a sharp B pencil, and then tone over everything with the broad point to get the background gray. Be careful, however, to leave little white slivers where features of the same tone overlap, such as at the cat's left cheek and where the leg comes up into the body. These white slivers should be toned last, when you can see the tones beside them and can keep them light enough so that they are not lost. Drawings of dark cats need these highlights to get the form across.

**Figure 7–18
A pencil drawing of
a striped cat.**

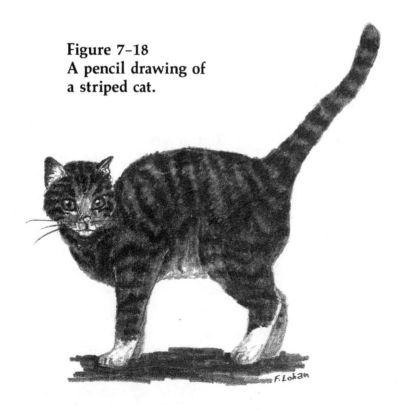

A

B

C

D

Figure 7-19
To complete your drawing of the striped cat, (A) lightly indicate the location of each stripe. (B) Use your sharp B pencil to draw the black stripes and the darks around the eyes. (C) Use the same B pencil to darken the gray areas, but leave white slivers where the cheek overlaps the shoulder and where the leg overlaps the chest. Leave the eyeball white also until the rest of the gray is complete. (D) Lightly tone the eyes and the white slivers you left on the cheek and upper leg. A dot of white gouache paint adds the eye highlights and several strokes with a sharp B pencil complete the whiskers.

LESSON 15
Pencil Drawing of a Black Cat

Tools and Materials
Sharp B and broad-point 6B, 3B, and B pencils; seventy-pound vellum-finish paper; kneaded eraser.

Procedure
Transfer a copy of figure 7-13 to your paper and follow the suggestions accompanying figure 7-21 to complete the

drawing of the black cat. As you work on your drawing, refer to figure 7-20 to guide your toning. As with the previous subject, the little white slivers that show the contour of the cat's left cheek and its leg should be toned last. Make the slivers gray enough to suggest black fur with some highlights on it but not so dark that all features disappear into one black mass.

Figure 7-20
A pencil drawing of
a black cat.

Figure 7-21
To complete your drawing of the black cat, (A) use a 3B pencil to darken the head, ears, and body, but leave white slivers where the face overlaps the shoulder and where the upper leg overlaps the chest. For the moment leave the eyeballs white also. (B) Use a B pencil lightly to cover up the white slivers, the eyeballs, and the chin. Rub a 6B pencil over the body to cover any stroke marks, but don't cover those white slivers where one part overlaps another. Add the whiskers with a sharp B pencil, and put a dot of white gouache paint on each eye.

LESSON 16
Pen Drawing of a Striped Kitten

Figure 7-22
A pen drawing of a striped kitten. I used my finest pen, a 5×0 technical pen, for this drawing.

Tools and Materials
Fine-point pen (I used my 5×0 technical pen, the finest point I have); seventy-pound smooth paper.

Procedure
Figures 7-22 through 7-24 should be used as references in this lesson. After inking in the outline (see figure 7-24A),

you will complete the drawing of this subject in basically two steps. First hatch in the dark stripes in the direction of the fur (figure 7-24B), and then hatch over the entire cat (figure 7-24C) to add gray stripes in between the dark ones and to darken the dark stripes. The darker stripes tend to disappear during this

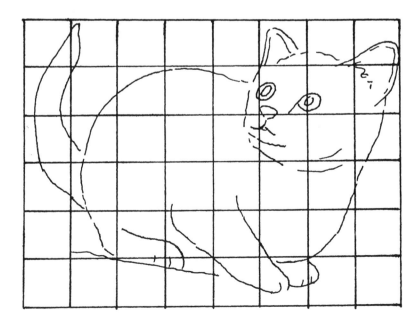

Figure 7-23
The gridded composition outline for Lesson 16.

hatching, so you may have to darken them a little more as you go over them and the adjacent areas.

When you hatch the eyeballs do not put the hatch marks too close together or you will make the eyes too dark. This drawing is large enough so that white space can be left in each eye as highlights—you won't have to paint it in.

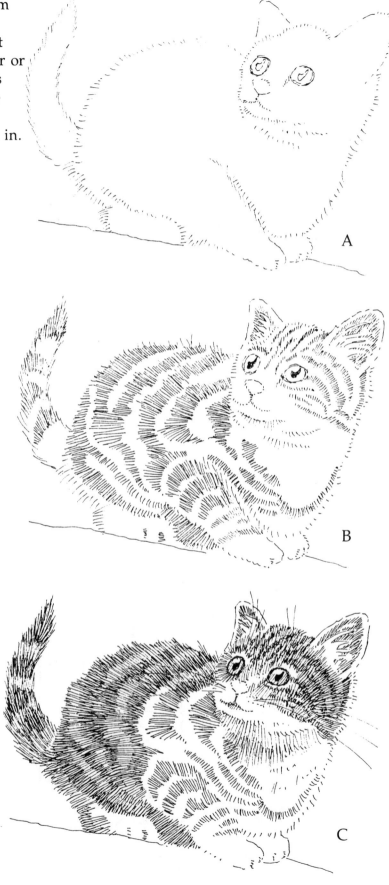

Figure 7–24
To complete the drawing of the striped kitten, (A) indicate the outline of the kitten with hatch marks and then erase all of the pencil guidelines. (B) Hatch the ears and all of the dark stripes. Be sure to place the hatch marks close together, making the lines go in the direction of the fur. (C) Hatch the gray stripes but run the new hatch lines right over the original ones to make them darker. Hatch the eyeballs with lines spaced a little farther apart, leaving the white highlight on each eye. Add eyebrow hairs and a few whiskers.

Six Pencil Studies of Short- and Long-Haired Cats

Figure 7-25
Six pencil studies of
short- and long-haired cats.

Tools and Materials
Sharp B pencil; seventy-pound vellum-finish paper; kneaded eraser.

Procedure
This set of exercises will give you some practice in using the grid system to copy a drawing and will also give you practice in making quick pencil sketches of simple cat studies. Figure 7-25 is your guide as you draw six different white cats in various interesting poses. To begin, copy

and transfer the gridded composition outlines in figure 7-26 to your paper, following the instructions in Chapter 2, and then pencil them in with a B pencil. Refer to figure 7-25 as you complete your drawings.

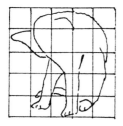

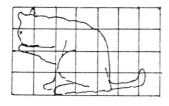

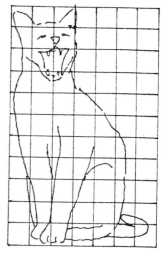

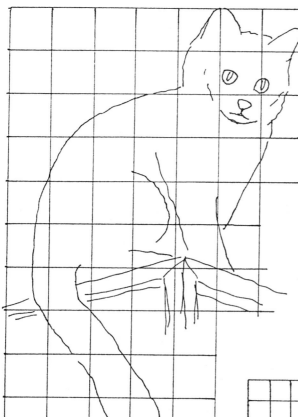

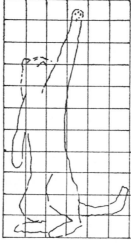

Figure 7-26
The gridded composition
outlines for the six cat studies
of figure 7-25.

LESSON 18
Changing an Outline

Tools and Materials
HB pencil; fine-point pen; tracing and seventy-pound smooth paper.

Procedure
Figure 7-27 is a pen outline of a short-haired cat that I drew by modifying the long-haired cat outline in figures 7-25 and 7-26. The adjustments I made are shown in figure 7-28, in which I suggested a slimmer cat inside the long fur outline of the original drawing—but I left the eyes and nose as in the original. To do this lesson, place your tracing paper over figure 7-28 and trace the dotted outline that represents the adjusted outline of the cat. Then blacken the back of the tracing paper and transfer this outline to your paper, following the instructions in Chapter 2.

Now ink in the study, using figure 7-27 as your guide. You should experiment with making small changes to some of your cat figures just to get some practice at making alterations. Not all of them will work out, and even those that don't will teach you valuable lessons.

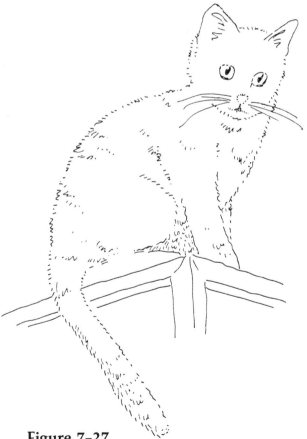

Figure 7-27
A short-haired cat drawn from the outline of the large, long-haired cat in figure 7-25.

Figure 7-28
This shows how I compensated for the long fur to get a working outline for the short-haired cat from the outline of the long-haired one.

LESSON 19
Pencil Drawing of a Striped Cat

Tools and Materials
Broad-point B pencil; seventy-pound
vellum-finish paper; kneaded eraser.

Procedure
Transfer another outline from the tracing
paper used in the previous lesson to a
fresh piece of paper. Following the same
sequence used in Lesson 14, use figure
7–29 as a guide to complete your
drawing. Remember, lightly indicate
where each stripe goes before darkening
the black ones. Then use the same B
pencil, but lightly, and go over the gray
areas as well as the dark stripes to
complete the cat's body.

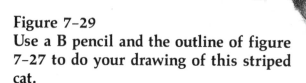

Figure 7–29
Use a B pencil and the outline of figure
7–27 to do your drawing of this striped
cat.

Summary

The thirteen lessons in this chapter gave
you some practice in suggesting various
fur patterns, from white through mottled
and striped to pure black, on both short-
haired and long-haired cats. You also saw
how you can take the posture from one
cat reference and create an entirely
different cat drawing. Mastering these
essential techniques will give you the
confidence to do your own drawings from
photographic references and from life.

8
Drawing Lions

Comparing Profiles

Three Pencil Studies of a Lion's Face

Pencil Study of a Lion

Pencil Study of a Lion Cub

Pen Drawing of a Lion Cub

Pencil Drawing of a Lioness on a Kill

Pen Drawing of a Lioness on a Kill

Walking Lion

Fine-Point Pen Study of a Sitting Lioness

Coarse-Point Pen Study of a Sitting Lioness

Comparing Profiles

The general shape and proportions of the lion's body (see figure 8–1) are very much like those of the house cat—to make a practical simplification. Note that the only real differences in these sketches are in the face, feet, and head. The ears are different, the eyes of the lion are smaller in proportion to its body, and the muzzles and feet are different.

The facial profile of the lion is based on three straight lines (see figure 8–2A), while that of the house cat is based on curved lines (figure 8–2B). The lion's body is about as thick as it is high off the ground; the length of the body is two-and-three-quarters squares, as shown in

figure 8–3. It can be very helpful if you take a pencil and some tracing paper and look for relationships such as these in photographs of any animals you want to sketch. An understanding of these relationships is a great asset when you want to make some adjustments to a pose that is "almost right but not quite" in your reference material.

In the case of lions, you can change a drawing of a lioness into one of a full-maned male lion by properly adding the mane, the fur under the belly, the fur on the elbows—and, of course, the tuft of hair on the end of the tail (figure 8–4).

Sketching on tracing paper placed over

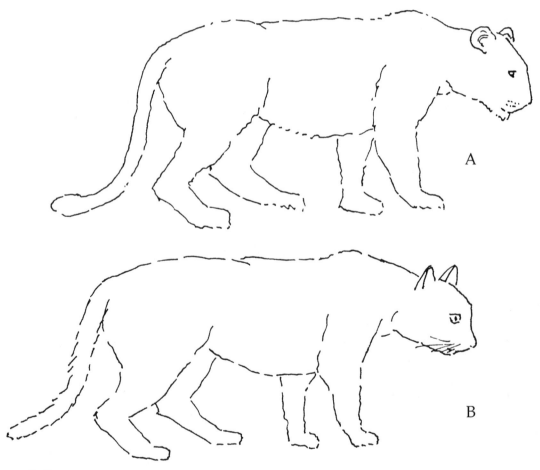

Figure 8–1
The body outlines of a lion, (A), and a house cat, (B), do not differ very much except for the ears, the profile of the head, and the relative size of the eyes and feet.

Figure 8-2
(A) The facial profile of a lion is characterized by straight lines; that of a house cat, (B), is characterized by curved lines.

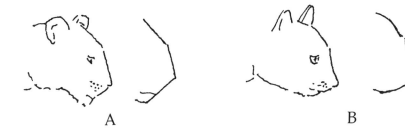

A   B

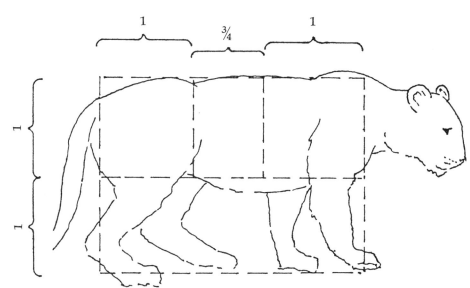

Figure 8-3
A lion's body is roughly as high off the ground as it is thick and is about two-and-three-quarters squares long.

A

B

Figure 8-4
Although a female lion's body is slightly less broad than a male's, a fairly accurate male lion can be drawn by adding a mane and other fur to the outline of a lioness. The mane and hair have been dotted over the outline of a lioness in A, and B is the resulting drawing of a lion.

some of your reference photographs can also be important in determining small things about your subject that will help make your subsequent drawings much more lifelike. Figure 8-5, for instance, shows a tracing-paper analysis of the front view of a lion's face. You can see that it is based on a circle, with the eyes on a line just a little above the center of the circle. Figure 8-6 is a quick pencil study drawn according to these observations. One of the important things to notice is that the tops of the

lion's eyes are horizontal, as you see in figure 8-7A, not slanted upward, as in figure 8-7B. Notice also that the lion's nose area is narrower halfway between the eyes and the tip of the nose—sort of a Coke-bottle shape. Little observations like these can make the difference between creating good and poor likenesses of the lion. You may often know that something is wrong with your composition sketch, but unless you are observant you may be unable to identify just what the problem is.

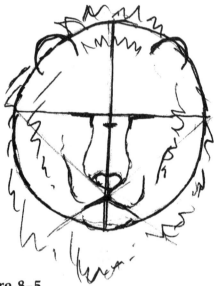

Figure 8-5
Tracing-paper analysis of the face of a lion from a photograph. The face is based on a circle, with the eyes located just above the center of the circle.

Figure 8-6
A drawing, made with a 3B pencil, that shows the proportions of figure 8-5.

A

B

Figure 8-7
The tops of the lion's eyes are horizontal, as in A, not slanted upward, as in B.

LESSON 20
Three Pencil Studies of a Lion's Face

Tools and Materials
Broad-point 4B and sharp B pencils;
seventy-pound vellum-finish paper, linen-
finish paper, coquille or any other highly
textured paper.

Procedure
Copy and transfer the drawing in figure
8–8 to a piece of vellum-finish paper,
following the instructions in Chapter 2.
Use figure 8–9 as a guide to do a broad-
point 4B pencil drawing of the lion's face,
using as few strokes as you can. Visualize
the light coming from the right side and
tone the left side of the drawing more
than the right. Notice how quickly you
can generate a reasonably good-looking
lion. Now take a sharp B pencil and
sharpen up the edges of some of the fur,

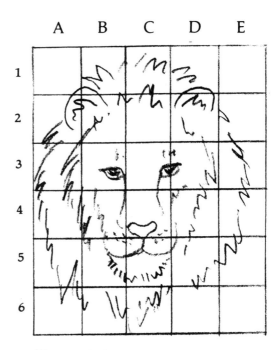

**Figure 8–8
The gridded composition
drawing of a lion's head.**

**Figure 8–9
A broad-point 4B pencil study
of the lion's head on vellum-
finish paper.**

using figure 8–10 as a guide. Be careful
not to overdo the sharpening; remember
that the essence of the lion is already in
place before the sharpening starts.

Now transfer a copy of your
composition to a piece of linen-finish
paper and use the broad-point 4B pencil
again—but this time use figure 8–11 as a
guide. See how the finish on the paper
creates an interesting effect in the dark
areas.

Any textured paper can be used to
create interesting effects in dark passages
when broad-point pencils are used. Figure
8–12 shows the same study done on
coquille paper, a paper with a very
pronounced pebbly finish. Do some
experimenting of your own with various
textured papers.

Figure 8–10
A broad-point 4B pencil study. Some edges were sharpened up with a sharp B pencil.

Figure 8–11
A broad-point 4B pencil study on linen-finish paper.

Figure 8–12
A broad-point 4B pencil study on coquille paper (paper with a pebbly finish).

LESSON 21
Pencil Study of a Lion

Tools and Materials
3B broad-point pencil; seventy-pound vellum-finish paper.

Procedure
Copy and transfer figure 8–13 to your working paper. I used one-half-inch squares for my drawing. Use figure 8–14, the completed study, as a guide, following the suggestions accompanying figures 8–15 and 8–16. Remember to keep the tops of the lion's eyes level rather than slanting upward.

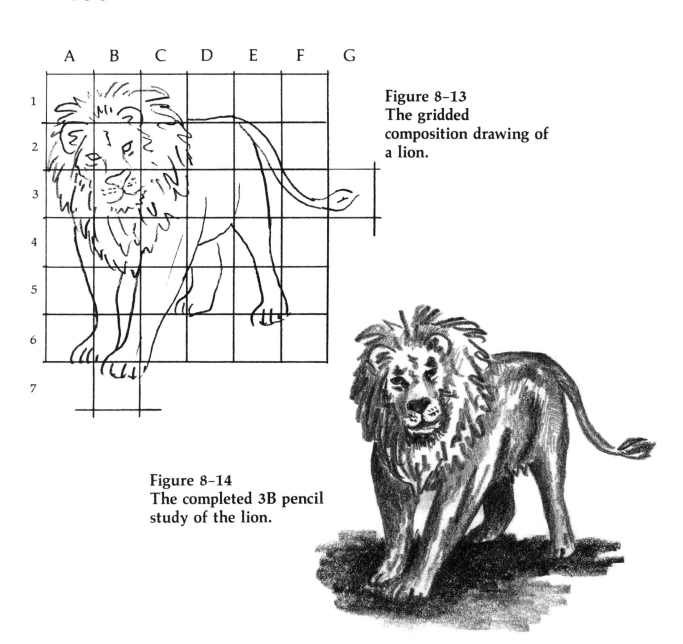

Figure 8–13
The gridded composition drawing of a lion.

Figure 8–14
The completed 3B pencil study of the lion.

Figure 8–15
Your first step is to indicate the body outline and mane with a 3B pencil. Use the sharp edge to do the eyes and the broad surface to do the remaining outlines.

Figure 8–16
Using the broad surface of the pencil, add the toning, being careful to leave some white highlights to help define the shape of the face and body.

LESSON 22
Pencil Study of a Lion Cub

Tools and Materials
Sharp B pencil; seventy-pound vellum-finish paper; kneaded eraser.

Procedure
Copy and transfer the outline of figure 8–17 to your working paper, referring to Chapter 2 for instructions if necessary.

Figure 8–18 shows the completed pencil drawing, which should be used as a guide as you follow the instructions accompanying figures 8–19 through 8–23.

Start with a sharp B pencil, and do the eyes and sharper facial features before the point starts to get significantly broader from wear. Be sure to leave a little white highlight in each eye. The last thing to do is the dark area under the board on which the cub is lying. Notice the individual broad strokes of the pencil in this area in figures 8–18 and 8–23.

If any area gets too dark, just touch it with the kneaded eraser to lighten it.

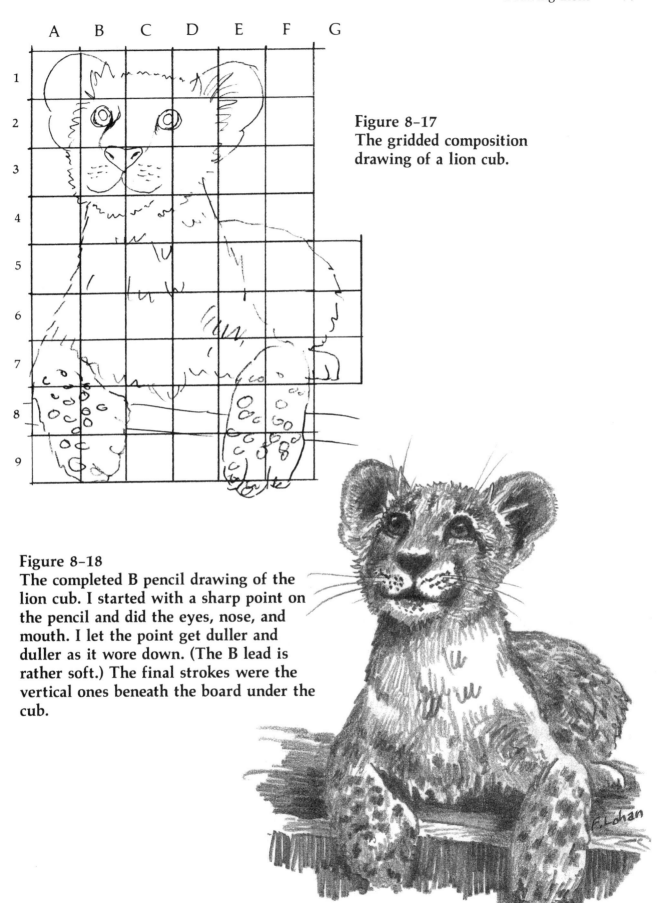

Figure 8-17
The gridded composition drawing of a lion cub.

Figure 8-18
The completed B pencil drawing of the lion cub. I started with a sharp point on the pencil and did the eyes, nose, and mouth. I let the point get duller and duller as it wore down. (The B lead is rather soft.) The final strokes were the vertical ones beneath the board under the cub.

Figure 8–19
Start with the eyes while the B pencil is still sharp. Be sure to leave the little white highlight on each eye. Then establish the furry outline and the whisker spots.

Figure 8–20
Begin to tone the darker areas on the ears, face, and neck. Carefully tone the light parts of the eyes, but leave the highlights alone.

Figure 8–21
Use the flat, worn part of the B pencil to lightly tone over the dark markings. Let most of the individual strokes show to help suggest fur. Be sure to leave white paper around the muzzle. If the eyes appear too light when you finish the face, darken them a little.

Figure 8–22
First show the darker spots on the legs and body.

Figure 8–23
Lightly tone over the spots, leaving some white highlights to help establish the appearance of roundness.

LESSON 23
Pen Drawing of a Lion Cub

Tools and Materials
Fine-point pen (I used my 3×0 technical pen); seventy-pound smooth paper (vellum-finish paper will work as well).

Procedure
If you have just done the previous lesson, transfer another copy of figure 8–17 to your working paper. If you have not done the previous lesson, copy and transfer the outline of figure 8–17 to your paper, according to the instructions in Chapter 2.

The completed pen drawing is shown in figure 8–24. This should guide your work as you follow the instructions accompanying figures 8–25 through 8–29.

Be careful as you do the eyes; don't put the hatch marks too close together or you will make the eyes too dark (see C in figure 8–25). When you tone the inside of the ears, build up the toned area by clustering groups of short hatch marks together, as you see in figure 8–26 at A, B, and C. Do not overlap the clusters.

Follow the instructions in the captions to complete your drawing.

**Figure 8–24
The completed fine-point
pen drawing of the lion cub.**

Figure 8-25
First establish the furry outline. Then complete the eyes—see A, B, and C—and then the nose and mouth area.

Figure 8-26
Next start the shading and texturing of the fur. Do the ears by building up clusters of hatch marks, as at A, B, and C.

Figure 8-27
Be sure to leave some light highlights as you complete the texturing of the fur. Make the inner ears darker by drawing hatch marks over the first hatch-mark layer. Go in the same direction as in the first layer, as at A and B.

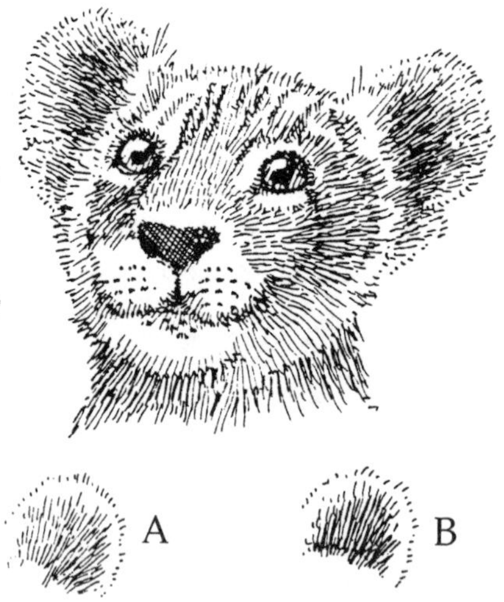

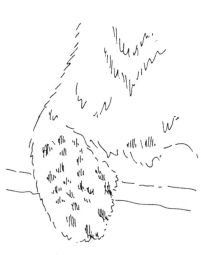

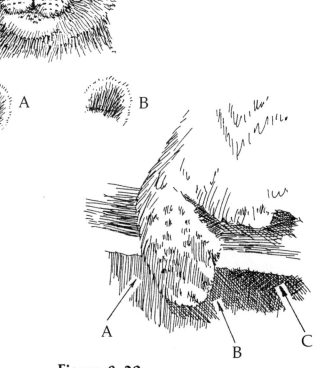

Figure 8-28
Put the major fur marks on the chest and the spots on the legs.

Figure 8-29
Hatch over the shaded fur areas, and then complete the board and the dark underside by hatching and crosshatching, as at A, B, and C.

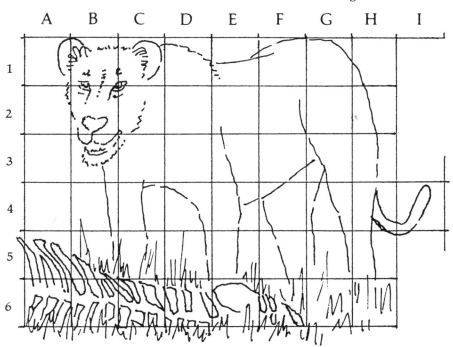

Figure 8-30
The gridded
composition drawing of
a lioness on a kill.

Pencil Drawing of a Lioness on a Kill

Tools and Materials
Sharp HB and broad-point 3B pencils;
seventy-pound vellum-finish paper;
kneaded eraser.

Procedure
Copy and transfer the outline of figure
8-30 to your working paper (see Chapter

2 for instructions if necessary). Then
follow the suggestions accompanying
figures 8-32 through 8-35 as you do
your drawing, using figure 8-31 as a
guide. Be sure that you leave some white
paper to represent the highlights on the
animal.

Figure 8-31
The completed HB and 3B
pencil drawing of the
lioness.

Figure 8-32
Start with a light pencil outline.

Figure 8-33
Use a sharp HB pencil to draw the eyes
and other facial features.

Figure 8-34
Use a broad-point 3B pencil to place the
dark features on the face and in the
shaded areas. Use the same pencil, but
lightly, to show the lighter tones of the
fur.

Figure 8-35
Use an HB pencil to darken the dead
zebra's stripes, as at A. Then use the
broad-point 3B pencil to darken them a
little more and to lightly tone the white
spaces between the dark stripes, as at B.

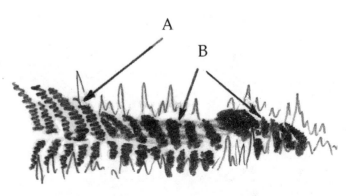

LESSON 25
Pen Drawing of a Lioness on a Kill

Tools and Materials
Fine-point pen (I used my 3×0 technical pen); seventy-pound smooth or vellum-finish paper.

Procedure
Transfer another outline of figure 8–30 to your working paper. Use figure 8–36, the finished pen drawing of the lioness, to guide your work as you finish your drawing of this subject, following the suggestions accompanying figures 8–37 and 8–38.

Figure 8–36
The completed 3×0 technical pen drawing of the lioness.

Figure 8–37
Start with an ink outline, and then add the facial features and some hatch marks to show the stripes on the zebra.

Figure 8–38
Crosshatch the stripes, as at A, and lightly hatch over the entire zebra, as at B. Carefully hatch the shaded parts of the lioness's body.

LESSON 26
Walking Lion

Tools and Materials
Sharp B pencil; seventy-pound vellum-finish paper; kneaded eraser.

Procedure
Copy and transfer the outline in figure 8–39 to your paper, according to the instructions in Chapter 2. Start with the eye, ear, and mouth while the pencil is still sharp, using figure 8–40 as a guide. Let the pencil get duller as you draw the mane; then tone the body. As the last thing, tone the shadow on the ground, using only horizontal strokes.

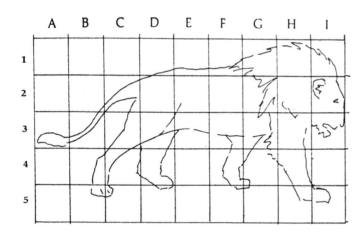

Figure 8–39
The gridded composition drawing for a small study of a lion.

Figure 8-40
The completed B pencil drawing of the lion.

LESSON 27
Fine-Point Pen Study of a Sitting Lioness

Tools and Materials
Fine-point pen (I used my 3×0 technical pen); seventy-pound smooth or vellum-finish paper.

Procedure
Copy and transfer the outline of figure 8-41 to your paper, referring to Chapter 2 for instructions if necessary.

Use figure 8-42, the completed pen sketch, as a guide. When you texture the lioness's body, use lines that more or less follow the direction of the fur on the animal.

Figure 8-42
The completed pen drawing of the seated lioness.

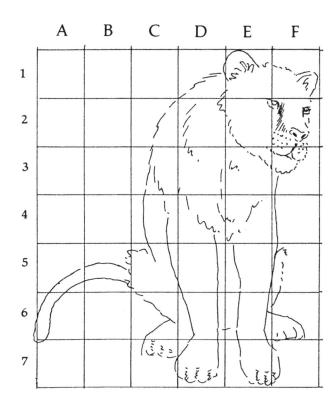

Figure 8-41
The gridded composition drawing of a seated lioness.

LESSON 28
Coarse-Point Pen Study of a Sitting Lioness

Tools and Materials
Coarse-point pen (I used my artist's fountain pen); seventy-pound smooth or vellum-finish paper.

Procedure
Transfer another copy of the outline in figure 8-41 to your paper and use figure 8-43 to guide your work. I used only vertical lines on the lioness and only horizontal lines on the ground. It is interesting to see how few lines can suggest the idea of the seated animal. In figure 8-44 I eliminated all outlines that were in the sunlight, letting only the shadows carry the form. This is often a good approach for poster work because the essence of the animal is retained, even at—or especially at—a distance. Prop the book up and look at this figure from across the room to see what I mean.

Figure 8-43
In making this two-tone study of the lioness, I worked quickly and used a fairly heavy pen point.

Figure 8-44
A sketch showing only the shaded areas on the lioness and some ground texture. The essence of the subject is still there.

9
Drawing Tigers

Proportions

Look at figure 9–1 to see the proportions of a tiger's body. It is about as high off the ground as it is thick, and it is about two-and-three-quarters squares long. The tiger's head is about three-quarters of a square long. Although these proportions are not anatomically exact, you can use them to quickly make reasonably accurate sketches of the animal.

The stripe pattern is unique to each tiger—it is said that no two tigers in the world have the same pattern. Sometimes the stripes are wide, sometimes narrow. Sometimes there are many, sometimes few. The stripe patterns can get quite intricate on the animal's face. Good reference photographs are essential when you try to draw your own tigers.

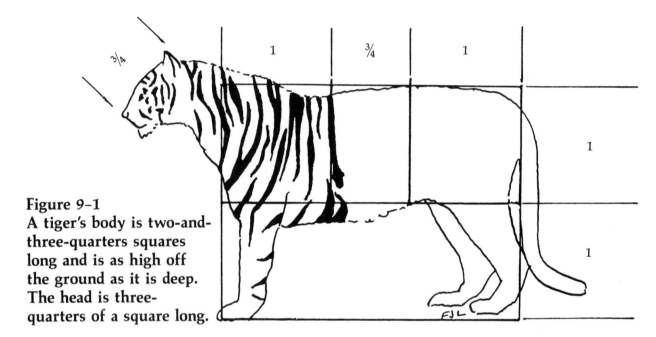

Figure 9–1
A tiger's body is two-and-three-quarters squares long and is as high off the ground as it is deep. The head is three-quarters of a square long.

LESSON 29
Pencil Sketch of a Tiger's Face

Tools and Materials
Sharp B pencil; seventy-pound vellum-finish paper; kneaded eraser.

Procedure
The tiger's face is basically circular, with the facial stripes primarily forming concentric circles, as you can see in figure 9–2. The eyes are located just above the

center of the circle, and the lower jaw is a little rectangle on the bottom of the circle.

Copy and transfer figure 9–3, the gridded composition drawing for this lesson, following the instructions in Chapter 2. This will give you a lightly drawn outline (which has been started in figure 9-4) of the major stripes and other facial features. Using a sharp B pencil, darken the stripes, as you see in figure 9-5. By the time you have completed the stripes, the point on your B pencil will have a broader spot. Use this spot to lightly tone the eyes and the orange parts of the fur—this has been started in figure 9-6.

The tiger's face has a lot of white fur; do not darken any of this. Carefully use the broad spot to complete the orange fur, using the completed sketch (figure 9-7) as your guide for the final toning. Don't forget the little white highlights in the eyes—these add sparkle to your sketch.

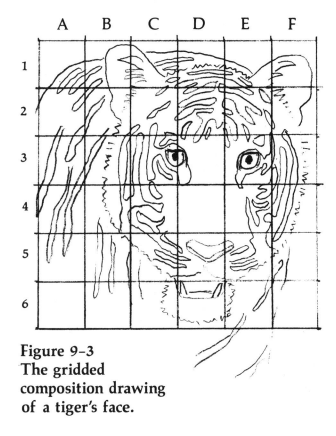

Figure 9-3
The gridded composition drawing of a tiger's face.

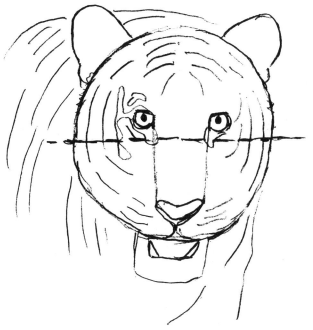

Figure 9-2
A tiger's face is based on a circle, with the eyes located just above the center. The jaw is a little rectangle at the bottom of the circle, and the facial stripes are mostly sections of concentric circles.

Figure 9-4
Start your drawing of the tiger's face by lightly indicating in pencil where all the features lie. The location of each of the major stripes should be indicated. The stripes are shown dark in this book only to ensure proper reproduction. Yours should be light.

Figure 9–5
First do the eyes with a sharp B pencil, but be sure to leave the little white highlights on the eyeballs. Then start to darken the stripes.

Figure 9–6
When all the stripes have been darkened, lightly tone the eyes, but leave the white highlights. Then darken the mouth, lips, and the orange fur.

Figure 9–7
When the orange fur has been toned, go over any of the dark stripes that may have become indistinct. Then add a few whiskers. This is the completed pencil drawing that should be used as a guide as you finish your drawing.

LESSON 30
Pen Sketch of a Tiger's Face

Tools and Materials
Fine-point pen (I used my 3×0 technical pen); seventy-pound smooth or vellum-finish paper.

Procedure
Transfer an impression of the gridded composition drawing of figure 9-3 to your paper and look at figure 9-10, your guide for this lesson. Start by putting in the details of the eyes, nose, and mouth, and then begin to darken the stripes (see figure 9-8). When the stripes have been hatched, refer to figure 9-9; crosshatch the stripes to make them darker and then hatch the orange areas of the fur. Add a few whiskers as the last thing. Your completed sketch should resemble figure 9-10. Be sure to leave the little highlight on each eye. If it gets lost you can reestablish it with a tiny drop of white gouache paint or typewriter correction fluid. Put it on with the tip of a toothpick—most brushes are too large to make a tiny dot.

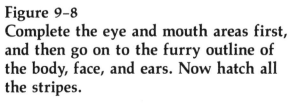

Figure 9-8
Complete the eye and mouth areas first, and then go on to the furry outline of the body, face, and ears. Now hatch all the stripes.

Figure 9-9
Crosshatch the stripes to make them darker, and then use short hatch marks to tone the orange fur. Leave the white patches of fur on the face untoned. Now lightly hatch the eyes (leaving the white highlights) and crosshatch the mouth.

Figure 9–10
This shows the completed pen drawing of the tiger's face, with the whiskers added. Use this figure to guide your work as you do your sketch.

LESSON 31
Pen Sketch of a Siberian Tiger

Tools and Materials
Medium-point pen (I used my artist's fountain pen); seventy-pound smooth or vellum-finish paper.

Procedure
Siberian tigers have much heavier coats than do the tigers that live in the steamy forests of India. The Siberian makes quite a handsome portrait. Copy and transfer the gridded composition drawing, figure 9–11, to your paper, according to the instructions in Chapter 2. Do the eyes, nose, mouth, and facial stripes, referring to figures 9–12 and 9–13. Be careful as

you work with the heavier pen point not to make the lighter fur too dark. Use figure 9–14, the completed pen sketch, as a guide while you make your drawing.

After the sketch was finished, I added the white highlights to the eyes with white gouache paint, applied with a toothpick. I used a very fine brush and white paint to show the whiskers where they cross the dark stripes on the tiger's face. Some white whiskers got too thick, so I simply used the pen to narrow them down after the paint had dried.

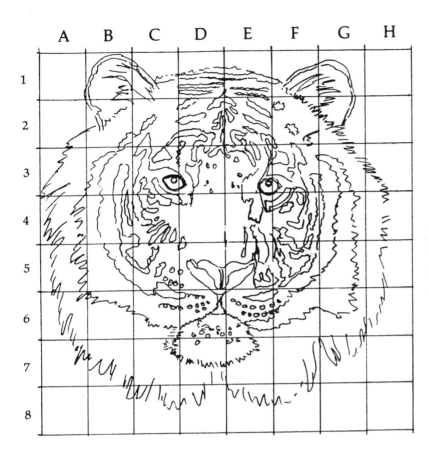

Figure 9-11
The gridded composition drawing of a Siberian tiger's face.

Figure 9-12
Start your sketch by doing the eyes, ears, and stripes.

Figure 9-13
(A) The stripes as initially toned with the pen. (B) Have each stripe look a little furry by making the edges less regular. (C) Lightly hatch the orange fur. Do not darken the white fur.

Figure 9–14
Use this completed pen drawing of the Siberian tiger to guide your work. The white highlights on the eyes were added by dots of white gouache paint applied with a toothpick. The white whiskers, where they cross the dark stripes, were also added with white gouache paint, applied with a fine brush. If they turn out too thick, thin them with ink after the paint dries.

LESSON 32
Pencil Sketch of a Siberian Tiger

Tools and Materials
Broad-point 3B and B pencils; seventy-pound vellum-finish paper; kneaded eraser.

Procedure
Transfer a copy of the gridded outline of figure 9–11 to your paper. Use figure 9–15, the completed pencil sketch, as a guide while you follow the instructions accompanying figures 9–16 through 9–18

to complete your sketch.

If some of your toning becomes too dark, lighten it by pressing the kneaded eraser to the area.

Just as I did on the previous sketch, I used white gouache paint, applied with a toothpick to do the white highlights on the eyes and applied with a fine brush to do the whiskers.

Figure 9–15
This completed pencil drawing of the Siberian tiger's face should be used as a guide. I used a broad-point 3B pencil for the stripes and a broad-point B pencil for the toning of the orange fur. The white whiskers were put in with a fine brush and white gouache paint and then made narrower with a pencil after the paint had dried.

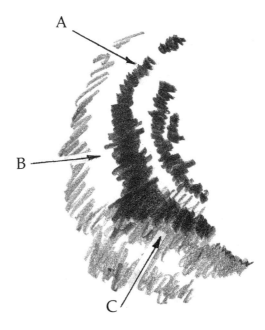

Figure 9–17
After the stripes are in place, as at A, make them look more furry, as at B, with a 3B pencil. Finally, lightly tone the orange fur areas with a B pencil, as at C.

Figure 9–16
First complete the eyes and the stripes with a 3B pencil.

Figure 9–18
Details of the mouth and chin areas. The light shading is done with a B pencil.

LESSON 33
Pen Sketch of a Standing Tiger

Tools and Materials
Fine-point pen (I used my 3×0 technical pen); seventy-pound smooth or vellum-finish paper.

Procedure
Copy and transfer the gridded outline drawing of figure 9–19 to your paper, following the instructions in Chapter 2.

Complete your sketch by using the drawing in figure 9–20 as a guide and following the same sequence of steps as in previous pen lessons. First do the eyes, nose, mouth, and the rest of the face. Then do the stripes, and finally carefully tone the orange fur.

When a subject, such as the tiger, is highly patterned, you often need few actual outlines to establish the form—the stripes, in this case, indicate the edges of the animal's body, as is evident in figure 9–21. Stylizing in this manner is often suitable for poster work.

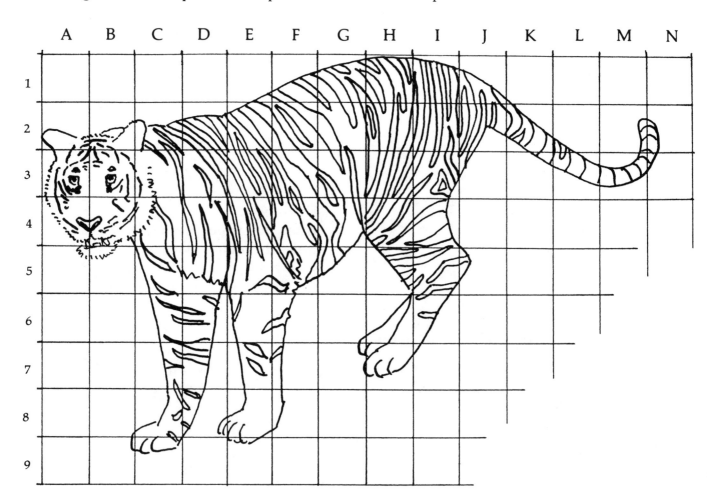

Figure 9–19
The gridded composition drawing of a standing tiger.

Figure 9-20
The completed pen drawing of the standing tiger. First do the eyes, ears, and mouth. Then put the stripes in place, and, finally, lightly hatch over the orange fur areas and draw the ground.

F. Lohan

Figure 9-21
When a subject, such as the tiger and some of the spotted cats, is highly patterned, the patterns alone carry the outline of the animal. There is sometimes no need to draw explicit outlines except where the pattern does not exist, such as on the legs in this stylized drawing of the tiger.

LESSON 34
Pencil Sketch of a Standing Tiger

Tools and Materials
Sharp 3B and broad-point B pencils; seventy-pound vellum-finish paper; kneaded eraser.

Procedure
If you have done the previous lesson, make another transfer of the gridded drawing of figure 9–19 to your paper. If you have not done the previous lesson, copy and transfer figure 9–19 by following the instructions in Chapter 2. Use figure 9–22, the completed pencil drawing, as a guide to complete your sketch.

As with previous sketches, complete the face first; do the eyes, nose, mouth, and facial stripes with the sharp 3B pencil. As the soft point wears down, it will become broader; do not resharpen it. Use it as it is to complete the stripes, following the instructions accompanying figure 9–23. Use a broad-point B pencil to tone the orange fur, going right over the black stripes (see figure 9–23).

Be sure to show the white fur on the face, chest, and underparts.

Figure 9–22
The completed pencil drawing of the standing tiger. Use a 3B pencil for the stripes and a B pencil for the tone on the orange fur and on the shaded areas.

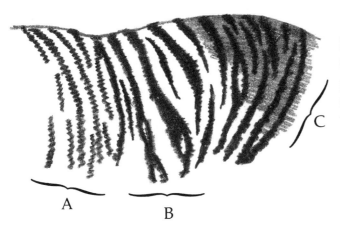

Figure 9–23
(A) Put the stripes in place with a 3B pencil. (B) Darken the stripes with the same pencil. (C) Tone the orange fur with a broad-point B pencil.

LESSON 35
Another Pencil Sketch of a Tiger

Tools and Materials
Sharp 3B and broad-point B pencils; seventy-pound vellum-finish paper; kneaded eraser.

Procedure
Copy and transfer figure 9–24 to your paper, according to the instructions in Chapter 2.

As in previous lessons, use a sharp 3B pencil to do the eyes, nose, mouth, and facial stripes first. Then do the body stripes, and finally use a broad-point B

pencil to tone the orange fur. Use the completed sketch, figure 9–25, as a guide.

An interesting exercise is to place a piece of tracing vellum—used as your final paper—over figure 9–24 and work directly on it with the pencils. When you use tracing vellum this way, you do not have to copy and transfer any sketches. If you back the tracing vellum with white paper, you can frame the result just as you would a drawing on heavier, opaque drawing paper.

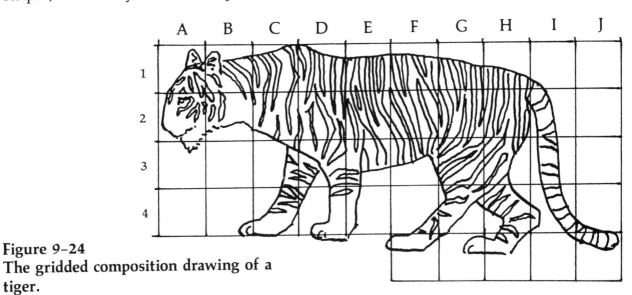

Figure 9–24
The gridded composition drawing of a tiger.

Figure 9-25
Use this completed pencil drawing of the walking tiger along with figure 9-24 and what you have already learned making pencil drawings of the tiger to complete your sketch of this subject.

Figure 9-26
The completed ink stipple drawing of the walking tiger. I used a fine point, my 3×0 technical pen.

LESSON 36
Ink Stipple Sketch of a Tiger

Tools and Materials
Fine-point pen (I used my 3×0 technical pen); seventy-pound smooth or vellum-finish paper.

Procedure
Copy and transfer figure 9–24 to your paper, referring to Chapter 2 for instructions if necessary.

Use the completed stipple sketch, figure 9–26, to guide your study of this subject as you follow the directions accompanying figure 9–27.

Ink stipple drawings can be reproduced very well in a reduced size. The open area between the dots is retained under conditions in which hatching tends to close up and become solid black. If severe reduction of your drawing is anticipated, it may be advisable to make a stipple drawing. Figure 9–28 illustrates this point. In figure 9–28A, figure 9–26 has been reduced to 65 percent of its original size. In 9–28B it has been reduced to 42 percent of its original size. You can see that the details held up very well without blending together. Remember this if you make sketches that you want to have printed on notepaper.

Figure 9–27
(A) Lightly dot in the outline, eye, and location of all stripes. Then erase all of the pencil guidelines. (B) Darken the stripes and make them the proper width. (C) Dot in the orange fur tones. Do not make this part so dark that the stripes become indistinct.

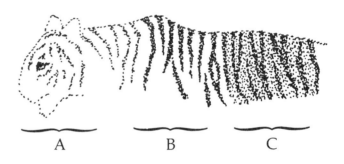

A   B   C

Figure 9–28
Ink stipple drawings hold up very well when reduced. In A you see the drawing in figure 9–26 reduced to 65 percent of its original size. The reduction in B is to 42 percent of its original size. Notice that very little detail was lost.

LESSON 37
Tiger Caricature

Making a caricature of something involves greatly exaggerating the subject's most characteristic features. Figure 9–29 shows, in A, a caricature of a tiger based to a large extent on the profile of the normal tiger shown in B. In doing the caricature I made the neck skinnier, really enlarged the lower jaw and the teeth, and enlarged the furry chin. Photographs show that when a tiger growls his nose wrinkles up (so that he can bare his upper teeth) and his ears go back; these features are incorporated in the caricature.

If you want to sketch my caricature, use the gridded outline drawing in figure 9–30.

Figure 9–29
The caricature shown in A is based on the properly proportioned drawing of B. I made the head larger, the neck longer and thinner, and the lower jaw and teeth much larger proportionately than life size. The tiger's ears are back and its nose wrinkled because this is what happens when a tiger (or any animal, for that matter) snarls.

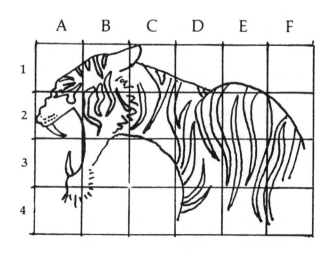

Figure 9–30
The gridded composition drawing of the tiger caricature.

LESSON 38
Another Tiger Caricature

A full-face caricature of a tiger, based on the circular pattern of a normal tiger's face, is shown in figure 9–31. In this case I again greatly exaggerated the size of the lower jaw and of the side facial fur. I also laid the ears back and wrinkled the nose.

Do this drawing yourself without a gridded outline. Use the circular facial layout of figure 9–31A to make in pencil

your own working drawing over which to put the ink.

When doing caricatures you can use the eyes to carry much, if not all, of the expression you want to convey. See figure 9–32 for some of the emotions that can be expressed simply by how the eyes are drawn.

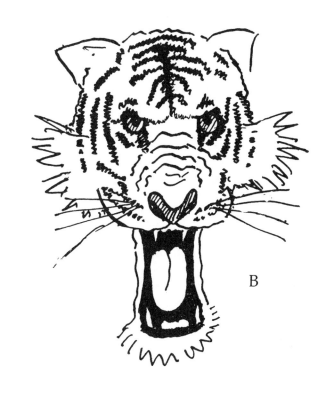

Figure 9–31
The front-view caricature of a tiger's face (B) is based on the properly proportioned sketch in A. The primary exaggeration is in the lower jaw and the side fur on the face.

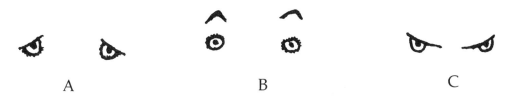

Figure 9–32
When you are caricaturing, let the eyes express emotion: the eyes in A show sadness; in B, surprise; in C, anger.

10
Sketching Leopards

Proportions

The body proportions of the leopard differ somewhat from those of the common house cat. Figure 10-1 shows that the leopard's body is two-and-three-quarters squares long and about three-

quarters of a square off the ground. Proportionally, this makes its body a little lower and a little longer than a cat's. Check figure 6-12 to see the proportions of a typical house cat.

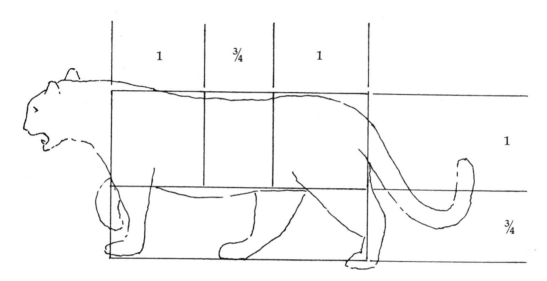

Figure 10-1
The approximate body proportions of a leopard.

LESSON 39
Pen Sketch of a Walking Leopard

Tools and Materials
Fine-point pen (I used my 3×0 technical pen); seventy-pound smooth or vellum-finish paper.

Procedure
Copy and transfer figure 10-2 to your working paper, following the instructions in Chapter 2.

Use figure 10-3, the completed pen sketch of the leopard, as your guide when

you do your drawing of this subject. The spots on the leopard's back and sides are actually clusters, or rosettes, of dark spots surrounding a medium-tone center. When I did this drawing, I first indicated the dark spots, as you see in figure 10-4 at A. Then I toned them one at a time with a few strokes of hatching, as you see at B. This is a very small drawing, so I did not try to indicate where each spot is located in pencil before I started to do the pen work. I just carefully drew the spots inside the pencil outline of the cat's body, making sure that I didn't make them too large. I constantly referred to the photograph from which I was working as I did this drawing. As you do your sketch, be careful to leave white paper

between the spots so that they remain distinct and do not run into each other.

The spot pattern is so dense on the leopard that indications of the body outline are not necessary in most places—only where there are no spots, as on the face and belly.

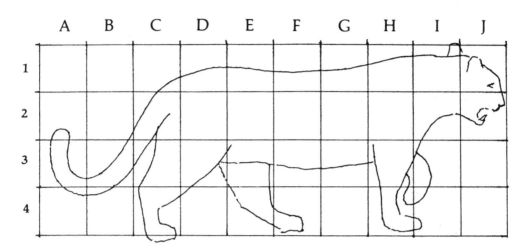

Figure 10–2
The gridded outline drawing of a walking leopard.

Figure 10–3
A 3×0 technical pen was used to make the completed pen drawing of the walking leopard.

Figure 10–4
(A) Each of the rosettes in the pattern is outlined with black spots. (B) The center of each rosette is lightly hatched with the pen to suggest the medium-dark tone.

LESSON 40
Pencil Study of a Walking Leopard

Figure 10–5
**The completed pencil drawing of
the walking leopard.**

Tools and Materials
Sharp 3B and broad-point B pencils;
seventy-pound vellum-finish paper;
kneaded eraser.

Procedure
Make another transfer of the outline in
figure 10–2 if you have done Lesson 39; if
not, then follow the instructions in
Chapter 2 to copy and transfer this
working drawing to your paper.

Figure 10–5 shows the completed pencil
drawing of the walking leopard; use it as
a guide as you do your pencil study of
this subject. As in the previous lesson,
the study is too small to make it
worthwhile to try to indicate the location
of all the spots before drawing them. The
result would be confusion on the paper. I
simply proceeded with my sharp 3B
pencil (I had to resharpen it several times
while doing this drawing) by indicating
the dark spots in each rosette, as you see
in figure 10–6 at A. Then, as you see in
figure 10–6 at B, I used my broad-point B

pencil to darken somewhat the center of
each rosette. I used the same B pencil to
tone the edges of the figure to give it
some three-dimensional feeling, as you
see at C. Finally, I did the ground with
my B pencil.

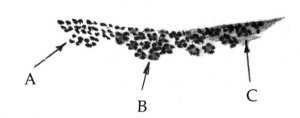

Figure 10–6
**(A) Use a sharp 3B pencil to draw the
black spots that outline each rosette in
the fur pattern. (B) Use a broad-point B
pencil to slightly darken the center of
each rosette. (C) Again use a broad-point
B pencil to lightly tone the edges of the
figure. This shading adds a roundness, or
dimension, to it.**

LESSON 41
Pen Portrait of a Leopard

Tools and Materials
Fine-point pen (I used my 3×0 technical pen); seventy-pound smooth or vellum-finish paper.

Procedure
Copy and transfer figure 10–7 to your working paper, following the instructions in Chapter 2. Unlike the drawings in the two previous lessons, this drawing is large enough to allow you to indicate in pencil where each spot lies before the inking is started.

Figure 10–8 shows the completed pen study of the leopard; use it as a guide. I

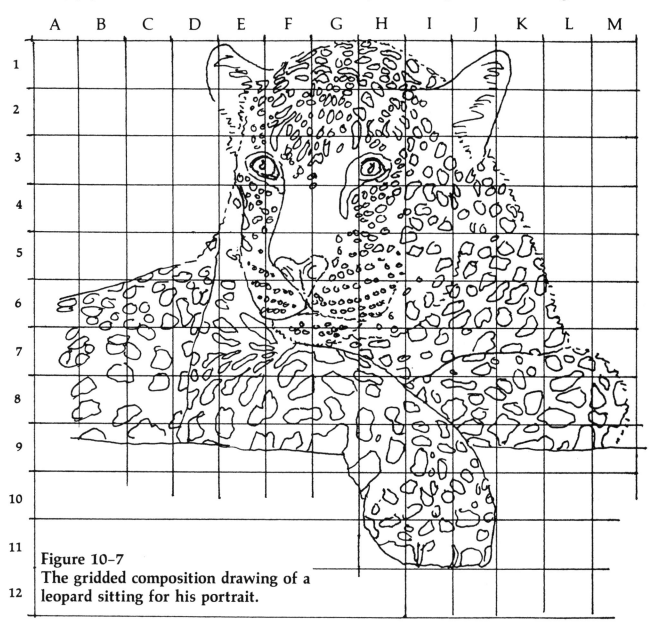

Figure 10–7
The gridded composition drawing of a leopard sitting for his portrait.

F. Lohan

**Figure 10-8
The completed fine-pen drawing of the
leopard, done with a 3×0 technical pen.**

usually start with an animal's eyes.
Figure 10-9 shows you the initial steps to
establish the eyes.

The primary steps in completing the
remainder of the drawing are shown in
figure 10-10. Indicate the outline and
hatch each of the spots; then erase all of
the pencil lines so that you do not smear
graphite all over your drawing as you
work. Crosshatch each spot to make it
darker, and then hatch the shaded areas.
In places where you need a darker tone,
such as around the eyes, crosshatch over
the hatching, as you see in figure 10-10.

In Chapter 9 it was demonstrated that
open ink work produced by stippling

reproduces quite well when it is reduced
in size. This holds true for any ink work
that is done in an open manner, in which
the lines are apart and distinct rather
than piled on top of one another to create
really dark darks. Figure 10-8, which is
an open drawing, is shown reduced in
size in figure 10-11. You can see how
well the line work held up when reduced
to 75 percent, and even to 50 percent of
its original size. The only parts of the
drawing that closed up—that is, became
solid black—are around the eyes, where
the lines were piled on top of one
another, and in a few of the spots.

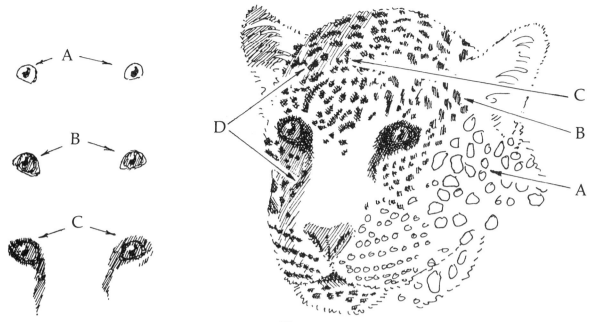

Figure 10-9
(A) Start the eyes this way. Plan here for the white highlight on each eye. (B) Develop the eyes further and lightly hatch over them, but leave the highlights. (C) Start the dark around the eyes by hatching with closely spaced lines.

Figure 10-10
(A) The light pencil circles from your transferred image determine the position and size of each spot. (B) Hatch each spot, and then erase the pencil marks. (C) Crosshatch each spot to make it darker. (D) Hatch right over the spots to indicate the shaded parts of the fur. Crosshatch around the eyes.

Figure 10-11
Open pen work will survive considerable reduction before the lines start to run together and produce solid blacks. These reductions of the drawing in figure 10-8 are 75 percent and 50 percent of the original size.

LESSON 42
Pencil Portrait of a Leopard

Figure 10–12
The completed pencil portrait of the leopard. A 3B pencil was used for the spots and a B pencil for the shading.

Tools and Materials
Broad-point 3B and broad-point B pencils; seventy-pound vellum-finish paper; kneaded eraser.

Procedure
Your reference for doing this pencil study is figure 10–12, the completed pencil portrait of the leopard. Copy and transfer figure 10–7 to your working paper,

referring to Chapter 2 if necessary.

As usual, I started by doing the animal's eyes, as you see in figure 10–13. Repeat these steps as you do your study of this subject. When you do the tone work that gives the animal some dimension, or roundness, do it carefully. If you get the tone a little too dark, just shape the kneaded eraser and press it to the area to lighten it somewhat. Be sure that you immediately knead the dirty part of the eraser into the inside before you use it again to lift off more graphite. If you don't, you may print a little stain where you do not want it, or you may dirty your fingers and get smudges on your paper from them.

When you do the animal's spots, use some side-by-side strokes of the pencil so that you get a sort of furry impression in the spots. They will look a lot more natural that way. If you make them sharp edged, they will look as if they were painted on the leopard. Figure 10–14 demonstrates these effects.

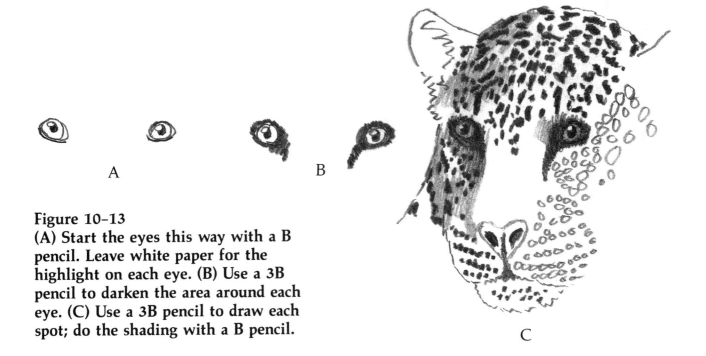

Figure 10–13
(A) Start the eyes this way with a B pencil. Leave white paper for the highlight on each eye. (B) Use a 3B pencil to darken the area around each eye. (C) Use a 3B pencil to draw each spot; do the shading with a B pencil.

Figure 10–14
(A) Do not make the spots look as though they were painted on the animal. (B) Make each spot suggest fur by drawing it with a group of parallel lines.

LESSON 43
Pencil Study of a Crouched Leopard

Tools and Materials
Sharp B and broad-point HB pencils; seventy-pound vellum-finish paper; kneaded eraser.

Procedure
Copy and transfer the outline of figure 10–15 to your paper, following the instructions in Chapter 2.

Figure 10–16 shows the completed pencil drawing, which should be used as your reference as you complete your drawing of this subject.

This is another rather small sketch, so place the spots using a sharp B pencil, without trying to lightly draw them first. Make the spots with very small side-by-side strokes so that you get a furry texture rather than the painted-on look you might get by drawing little circles and filling them in. Do the toning, which gives a third dimension to your drawing, with an HB pencil. Use your kneaded eraser to lighten some areas if your toning gets too dark; just press it on the dark place and lift off the graphite.

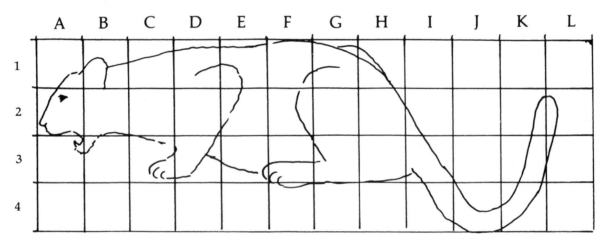

Figure 10–15
The gridded outline drawing of a crouching leopard.

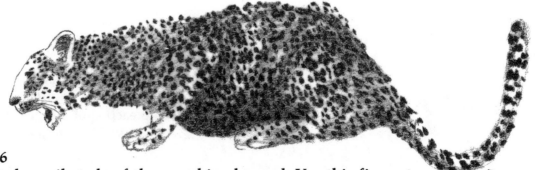

Figure 10–16
The completed pencil study of the crouching leopard. Use this figure to guide you as you complete your study of this subject. Use a sharp B pencil for the spots and an HB pencil for the shading.

11
Sketching Cheetahs

Proportions
Walking Cheetah
Running Cheetah
Standing Cheetah

Proportions

The cheetah, the fastest animal on four feet, is a lean and lanky cat. Figure 11-1 shows the approximate body dimensions of the cheetah—it has a body that is three squares long and about one-and-three-quarters squares off the ground.

LESSON 44
Walking Cheetah

Tools and Materials
Fine-point pen (I used my 3X0 technical pen); seventy-pound smooth or vellum-finish paper.

Procedure
Copy and transfer the composition drawing in figure 11-2 to your paper by following the steps in Chapter 2. This drawing is large enough to allow you to indicate in pencil every spot to be included on the animal. Note that the tail is only partly spotted—the last portion has stripes.

A completed pen stipple drawing of the subject is shown in figure 11-3. This will be your guide as you follow the instructions in figures 11-4 and 11-5 to complete your own drawing.

Start by lightly outlining the cheetah and showing the facial features and spots with ink dots, as you see in Figure 11-4A. When this is all done, erase the

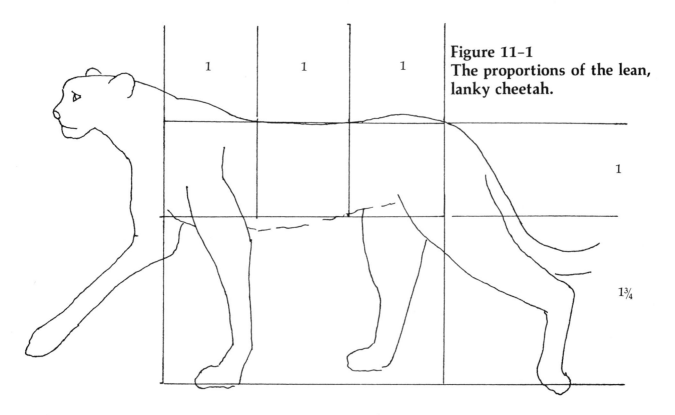

Figure 11-1
The proportions of the lean, lanky cheetah.

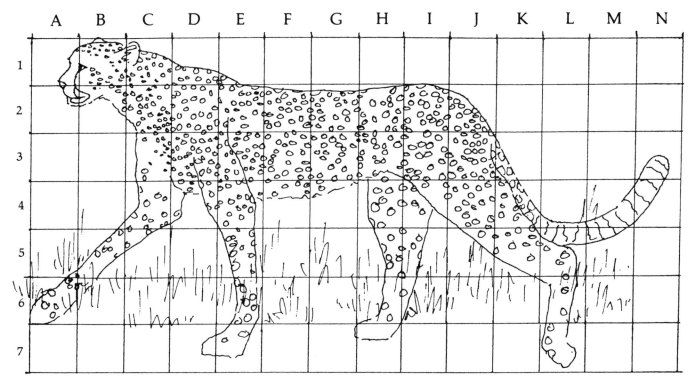

Figure 11–2
The gridded composition drawing of a
walking cheetah.

Figure 11–3
The completed pen stipple drawing of the
walking cheetah. Use this figure as a
guide as you follow the instructions to
do your drawing.

pencil lines from your transferred drawing so that you do not smear graphite on your drawing as you work. Next bring each spot up to size by adding stipple dots as needed. Also add the facial stripe from the eye toward the mouth (see figure 11-4B). Now, as you see in figure 11-4C, carefully, and lightly, stipple around the outer edges of the figure to suggest some roundness and three-dimensional form.

Do not put any tone on the lower legs. The legs will disappear when the ground is stippled in if they have been toned. Be careful not to overdo the stippling because you cannot erase or remove the dots once they are on the paper. If any of the spots seem to disappear as you are stippling, just darken them with more dots.

To draw the ground on which the cheetah stands, follow the instructions accompanying figure 11-5. Dot in the rock shapes, as in 11-5A, and then do the shading under the rocks and start the grass tone, as in 11-5B. Finally, add a few tall sprigs of grass that go right over the legs, as in 11-5C. You can see that if the legs were also of a dark tone they would blend right into the ground and grass tone and become indistinct. The legs remain untoned where they overlap the ground.

Figure 11-4
(A) Dot in the cheetah's outline and indicate in ink where each spot lies. Then erase all of the pencil guidelines. (B) Complete the stippling of the eye, nose, and facial pattern, and then bring each spot up to full size and tone. (C) Add some roundness to the body by lightly stippling the outer edges of the body and all shaded areas, except for the lower legs.

 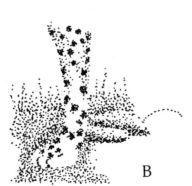 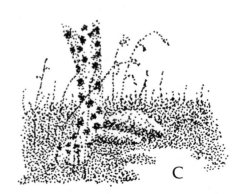

Figure 11-5
(A) Dot in the major rocks. (B) Do the ground and grass, but do not put any dots on the legs where they overlap with the ground. (C) Complete the stippling of the ground and add a few sprigs of grass right over the legs.

LESSON 45
Running Cheetah

Tools and Materials
Sharp B and sharp and broad-point HB
pencils; seventy-pound vellum-finish
paper; kneaded eraser.

Procedure
Follow the instructions in Chapter 2 to
copy and transfer the composition
drawing, figure 11–6, to your paper.
Show the location of each spot on this
drawing.

Use figure 11–7, the completed pencil
drawing of the running cheetah, to guide
your pencil work as you do your study of
this subject. As usual, start with the face
and mouth area, as you see in figure
11–8A. Use a sharp B pencil and let it get
duller and duller as you do the spots. You
first need the sharp point to get the eyes,

nose, and mouth parts, but the duller
point is better to draw the spots. Fill in
with extra spots where needed and add a
few lighter spots to the forehead and
chin, as shown in figure 11–8B. Hold
your drawing out at arm's length to
evaluate the spot distribution and density.
Start to tone the outer edges of the figure
to give it some roundness and sharpen
any fuzzy edges with a sharp HB pencil.
All this is illustrated in figures 11–8B and
11–8C. Now use your kneaded eraser by
just touching it to the face area to lighten
the tone a bit, but leave the sharp edge,
as you see in figure 11–8D.

Use a B pencil to draw the ground
under and around the cheetah (see figure
11–7).

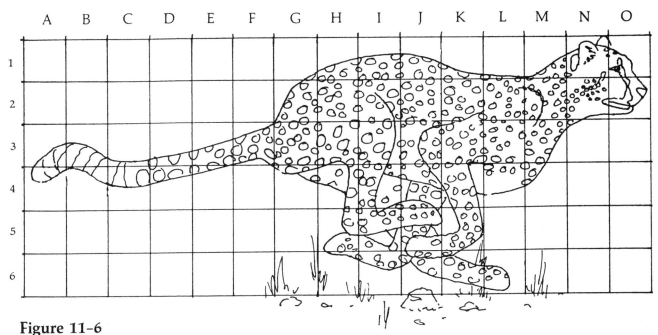

Figure 11–6
**The gridded composition drawing of a
running cheetah.**

Figure 11-7
The completed pencil sketch of the
running cheetah. Use a B pencil to draw
the black spots and an HB pencil to do
the toning on the body. Use the B pencil
to draw the ground.

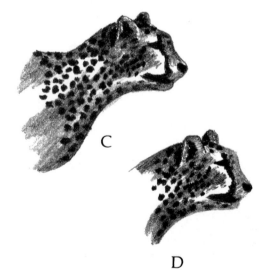

Figure 11-8
(A) Start by drawing the facial features
and the spots with a B pencil. (B) Fill in
where necessary with more spots. Then
start shading the edges of the figure and
add a few fainter spots to the chin and
forehead with an HB pencil.
(C) Complete the edge shading and
sharpen the outline where needed with a
sharp HB pencil. (D) Touch your kneaded
eraser to the edges of the forehead and
neck to lighten the tone—but keep the
sharp edges.

LESSON 46
Standing Cheetah

Tools and Materials
Sharp B (I used my mechanical pencil with a B lead) and 3B pencils; seventy-pound vellum-finish paper; kneaded eraser.

Procedure
Copy and transfer the outline drawing of figure 11–9 to your paper, following the instructions in Chapter 2.

Use what you have learned doing the

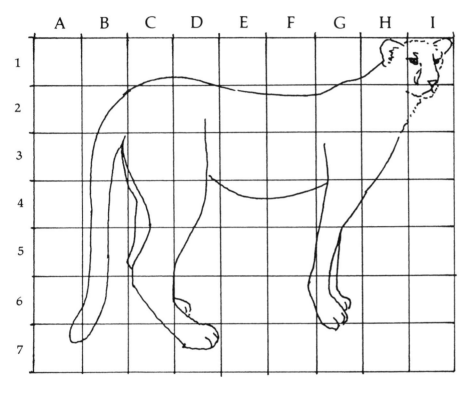

Figure 11–9
The gridded outline figure of a standing cheetah.

Figure 11–10
The completed pencil drawing of the standing cheetah was done with a mechanical pencil using a 0.5 millimeter lead. A 3B pencil was used for the ground.

Figure 11-11
The running cheetah of figure 11-7 is
drawn in ink with a 3×0 technical pen.

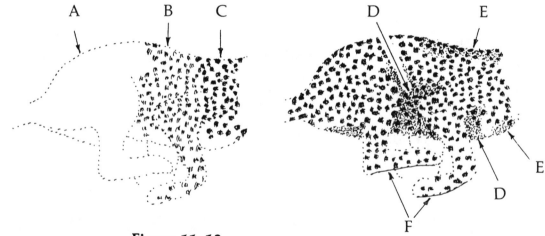

Figure 11-12
(A) Lightly dot the outline in ink, and
then erase the pencil lines from your
transferred outline. (B) Indicate the spots
on the entire animal. (C) Darken each
spot by crosshatching over it. (D) Stipple
the shaded areas that define the near
legs. Put no dots on the legs themselves
yet or they may disappear into the body.
(E) Stipple around the entire outline. (F)
If some edges appear indistinct, add
outlines. Do this only if absolutely
necessary.

previous pencil drawing of a cheetah, and other earlier pencil drawings, to do your own drawing of figure 11-10. Use a sharp B pencil and start with the face, do the spots, and finally tone the edges of the figure. Let the completed drawing in figure 11-10 guide your work. Use a 3B pencil to indicate the ground and shadow under the cheetah.

Drawing a Cheetah in Ink

The cheetahs drawn with pencil in lessons 45 and 46 can easily be drawn in ink also. Figure 11-11 shows the running cheetah of figure 11-7 drawn with a 3×0 technical pen. The steps to follow to do any of the cheetahs in ink accompany figure 11-12.

Be careful, when you are using ink, to draw the cheetahs so that you do not lose edges that are not outlined with an ink line. Such edges are shown at D in figure 11-12. You have only black-and-white marks to suggest different surfaces; at the places where adjacent or overlapping surfaces of the same color and texture must be made distinct from one another, you must slightly exaggerate or create tonal differences to achieve the necessary distinctions. If you do not do this, the surfaces will blend into one another and cause some visual confusion. In figure 11-11, it is only the darker body tone that allows you to see the two near legs where they cross the body. A few dots too many on the lighter legs would make them blend into the body. Work carefully with your stippling and take one area at a time when you come to places like this in your stipple drawings.

12
Sketching Other African Cats

Sketching a Caracal

Pen Drawing of a Serval

Another Pen Version of a Serval

Pen Stipple Drawing of a Serval

Two lesser-known African cats are the subjects of this chapter. The first, the caracal, is a small cat that is related to the lynx, as the ear tufts suggest. The second, the serval, is a shy, mostly nocturnal, cat.

LESSON 47
Sketching a Caracal

Tools and Materials
Broad-point B and sharp HB pencils; linen-finish paper; kneaded eraser. (If you do not have linen-finish paper, use vellum-finish paper. The only difference will be that the linen texture will not be present in your finished sketch.)

Procedure
Copy and transfer the gridded composition drawing of the caracal in figure 12–1 to your paper by following the instructions in Chapter 2.

If you use linen-finish paper for this study, your drawing, when completed, will resemble that in figure 12–2, with the linen texture showing in the dark areas. A drawing on vellum-finish paper, with no texture, will resemble figure 12–4. In either event, follow the instructions accompanying figure 12–3 to do your drawing, but use the appropriate completed drawing (figure 12–2 or 12–4) as your guide.

A broad-point B pencil will leave a somewhat rough outline on the figure, so the last step is to trim the outline up with a sharp HB pencil, as shown at the arrow in figure 12–3B.

If some of your pencil tone lines overlap a little, an unwanted dark mark may result. If this happens, just lightly touch the kneaded eraser to the area to make the tone smooth and uniform again.

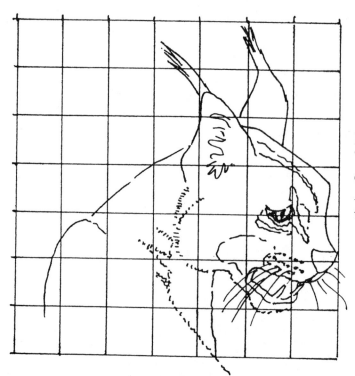

Figure 12–1
The gridded composition drawing of a caracal, an African cat that is related to the lynx.

Figure 12–2
A broad-point B pencil drawing of a
caracal done on linen-finish paper. Note
that the texture of the paper shows
clearly in the darker areas.

A   B

Figure 12–3
(A) Use a broad-point B pencil, pressing
heavily, to draw all of the dark features.
(B) Use the same pencil, but lightly this
time, to tone the lighter fur. Leave white
paper for the little white fur features.
Trim the edges of the outline smoothly
with a sharp HB pencil, as has been done
at the arrow.

Figure 12–4
A broad-point B pencil drawing of the
caracal on untextured vellum-finish
paper.

LESSON 48
Pen Drawing of a Serval

Tools and Materials
Fine-point pen (I used my 3×0 technical pen); seventy-pound smooth or vellum-finish paper.

Procedure
Using the instructions in Chapter 2, copy and transfer the composition drawing in figure 12–5 to your paper.

Note that in figure 12–6, the completed pen drawing of the serval, only diagonal lines were used, and all lines run in the same direction. Use figure 12–5 to guide your work as you follow the suggestions accompanying figures 12–7 and 12–8 to complete your study of the subject.

Note that no outlines are required because the tone you place over the entire figure defines the edges of the figure.

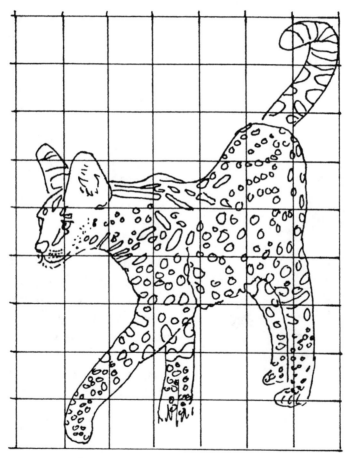

Figure 12–5
The gridded composition drawing of a serval, a small, secretive, nocturnal African cat.

Figure 12-6
A pen drawing of the serval containing only diagonal lines, all going in the same direction.

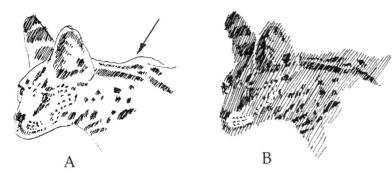

A   B

Figure 12-7
(A) Start by indicating all of the dark features within the pencil outline, which is shown at the arrow. (B) Hatch lightly right over the dark features to fill in the pencil outline completely; then erase the pencil lines.

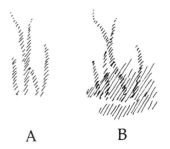

A   B

Figure 12-8
(A) Indicate a few individual grass sprigs under the serval. (B) Hatch the ground in the same direction and go right over the lower part of the grass sprigs.

LESSON 49
Another Pen Version of a Serval

Tools and Materials
The same as for Lesson 48.

Procedure
Transfer an outline of figure 12–5 to a fresh piece of paper. Then complete your drawing by following the instructions accompanying figure 12–10, using the completed drawing in figure 12–9 as your guide. As soon as you have indicated the outline and located all of the dark features in ink (as you see in figure 12–10A), erase the pencil guidelines so that the graphite does not get smeared over your drawing as you work.

A

Figure 12–9
A pen drawing of the serval with outlines, hatching, and crosshatching.

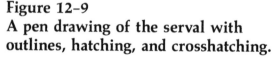

B

Figure 12–10
(A) Indicate the outline in ink by drawing a broken line, and then hatch all dark features. Now erase all pencil guidelines. (B) Hatch over the lighter fur areas, but leave some white paper showing on the muzzle and cheek.

LESSON 50
Pen Stipple Drawing of a Serval

Tools and Materials
The same as for Lesson 48.

Procedure
Transfer another copy of figure 12–5 to a
fresh piece of paper. Follow the
instructions accompanying figure 12–12,
using figure 12–11 as a reference, to
complete your pen stipple study.

In this lesson I used two different
vellum-finish papers: a hard-finish paper
for the completed drawing in figure
12–11 and a softer paper (actually a
copier paper) for the how-to sketches in
figure 12–12. Compare these illustrations
and you will see that the softer paper
allowed the ink to spread a tiny bit,
making dots noticeably larger than those
on the harder paper. Papers will vary and
to some degree will affect the appearance
of your completed drawings.

Figure 12–11
A pen stipple drawing of the serval.

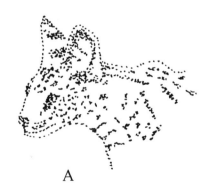

A

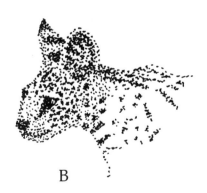

B

Figure 12–12
**(A) Dot in the outline and all dark
features, and then erase all pencil
guidelines. (B) Dot in the lighter fur
tone, and darken any of the dark spots
that seem to disappear.**

13
North American Cats

Proportions
Pen Drawing of a Mountain Lion
Sketching a Mountain Lion's Face
Pencil Drawing of a Bobcat

North America has a number of native nondomesticated cats, among them the mountain lion (also known as the panther and the cougar), the bobcat, and the lynx. This chapter will show you how to draw the first two. The lynx, which resembles the bobcat, is found farther north and has longer ear tufts and less prominent spots.

Proportions

The mountain lion has a small head in proportion to its body, which is about two-and-a-half squares long and is almost one square off the ground (see figure 13–1).

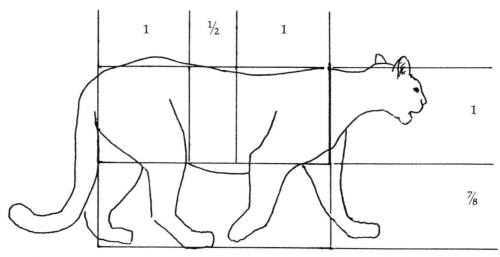

Figure 13–1
The proportions of a mountain lion, which is also known as a panther and a cougar in different parts of the country.

LESSON 51
Pen Drawing of a Mountain Lion

Tools and Materials
Fine-point pen (I used my 3×0 technical pen); seventy-pound smooth or vellum-finish paper.

Procedure
Follow the instructions in Chapter 2 to copy and transfer figure 13–2, the composition drawing, to your paper.

This study includes some of the typical rocky habitat of the western mountain lion. Both the animal and the cliff are rendered primarily in outline, with some

of the form and texture shown by hatching.

The cat is light in color, so there is little to draw except its outline, a few shaded areas, and fur indications.

Use the completed pen drawing, figure 13–3, to guide your pen work. Just take one element at a time and complete it. I started with the mountain lion, did the scrub growth under it, and then drew the rocks. This sketch shows how much can be suggested by a few pen lines.

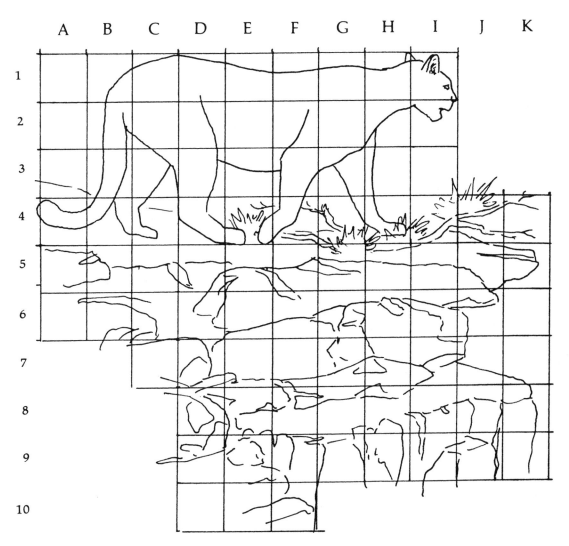

Figure 13-2
The gridded composition drawing of a mountain lion.

Figure 13-3
The completed pen sketch of the
mountain lion and some of his mountain
habitat. The simple outline approach
used in this lesson is one of the ways
that the pen is most effective.

LESSON 52
Sketching a Mountain Lion's Face

Tools and Materials
Fine-point pen (I used my 3×0 technical pen); seventy-pound smooth or vellum-finish paper.

Procedure
Copy and transfer the outline of the face in figure 13-4 to your paper, following the instructions in Chapter 2.

Use the completed drawing, figure 13-5, to guide your work as you follow the instructions accompanying figure 13-6. Keep your hatch lines short as you tone the lion's body. If an area must be darkened, put more hatch marks on top of the earlier ones after they have dried. I used a little crosshatching in the dark area of the mouth and on the nose.

Be sure to leave the little highlights in the eyes and some highlight on the nose to help suggest moist surfaces glistening in the light. The white parts of the lion's whiskers, where they cross the darker tones, were done with a fine brush and white gouache paint after the drawing was completed and the ink dry. The white paint made too wide a stripe as applied, so I waited until it dried and then I narrowed the white down with the pen (see the whiskers in figure 13-5).

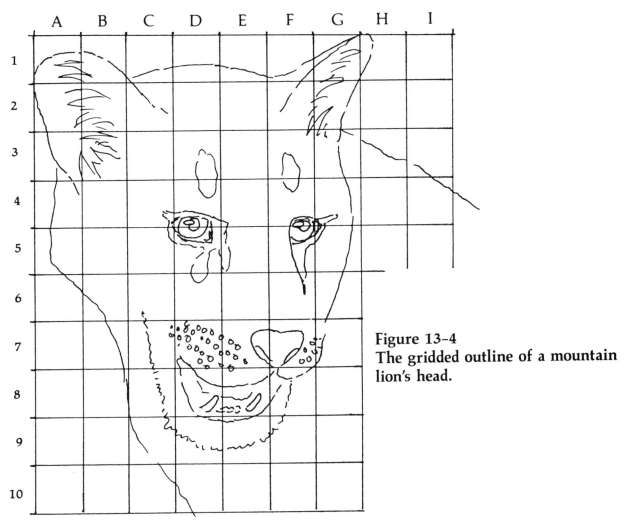

Figure 13-4
The gridded outline of a mountain lion's head.

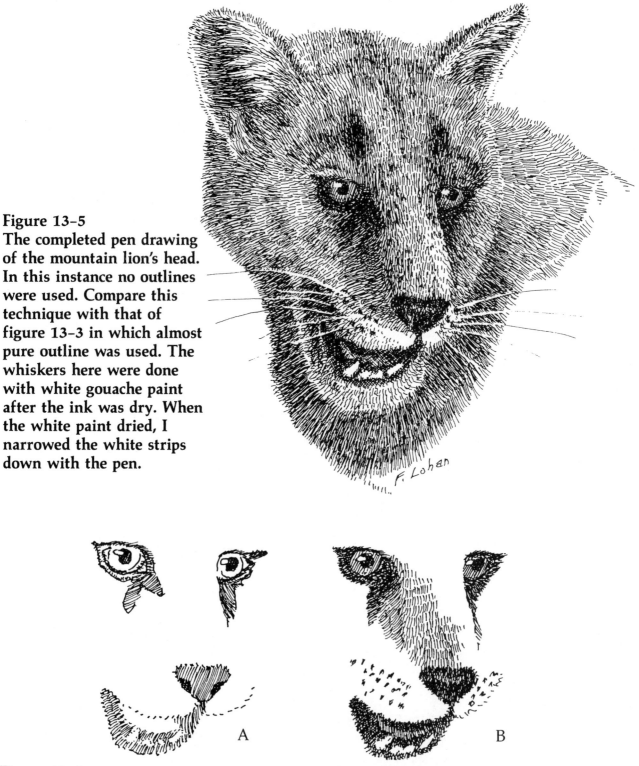

Figure 13-5
The completed pen drawing of the mountain lion's head. In this instance no outlines were used. Compare this technique with that of figure 13-3 in which almost pure outline was used. The whiskers here were done with white gouache paint after the ink was dry. When the white paint dried, I narrowed the white strips down with the pen.

Figure 13-6
To complete the mountain lion's face, (A) block in the dark areas of the eyes, nose and mouth by using closely spaced hatch marks. (B) Use both crosshatching and overhatching in the same direction to complete the darks. Then just hatch the light areas with short and evenly spaced lines, going over areas that should be a little darker.

LESSON 53
Pencil Drawing of a Bobcat

Tools and Materials
Sharp B and broad-point B pencils; seventy-pound vellum-finish paper; kneaded eraser.

Procedure
The bobcat's body is squat and short, as you see in figure 13–7. Use the instructions in Chapter 2 to copy and transfer the outline of figure 13–8 to your paper.

This is a very small drawing, so start out with a sharply pointed B pencil to do

the eyes, nose, and mouth details correctly. Now follow the instructions accompanying figures 13–10 and 13–11 while you use the completed sketch, figure 13–9, as a guide. Be sure to use your kneaded eraser as you go along if any of the areas or tones seem too dark. Just press it to the area to lighten the tone; do not rub it back and forth. You can do this two or three times to an area to lighten it.

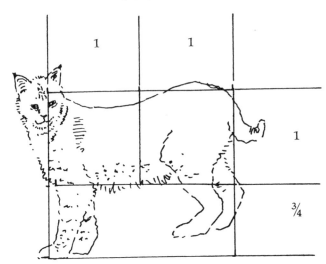

Figure 13–7
The proportions of a bobcat.

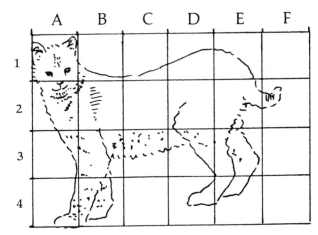

Figure 13–8
The gridded outline for a small sketch of a bobcat.

Figure 13–9
The completed pencil sketch of the bobcat.

A   B   A   B

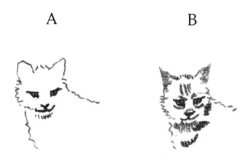

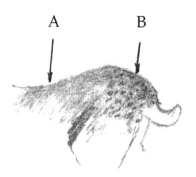

Figure 13–10
(A) Use a very sharp B pencil to indicate the eyes, nose, and mouth. (B) Add the remaining dark markings before you lightly tone over the head and body.

Figure 13–11
(A) Lightly tone the body with a broad-point B pencil. Press your kneaded eraser to the areas that appear too dark.
(B) When the tone is right, add some faint spots.

14
Sketching Central and South American Cats

Proportions
Pen Drawing of a Margay
Pencil Drawing of a Margay
Pencil Drawing of a Margay
  on Linen-Finish Paper
Pen Drawing of an Ocelot
Pen Sketch of a Jaguar
Pen Drawing of a Walking Jaguar

Proportions

The margay, one of the smaller Central and South American cats, is about three feet long and is proportioned differently from a house cat. In figure 14–1 you can see that the margay's neck, body, and tail are longer than the house cat's. The spots on the margay's coat are beautiful—they are outlined in a very dark brown or black, with the center of the patches a rich, chestnut brown. The fur is tan on top and on the sides with white underneath.

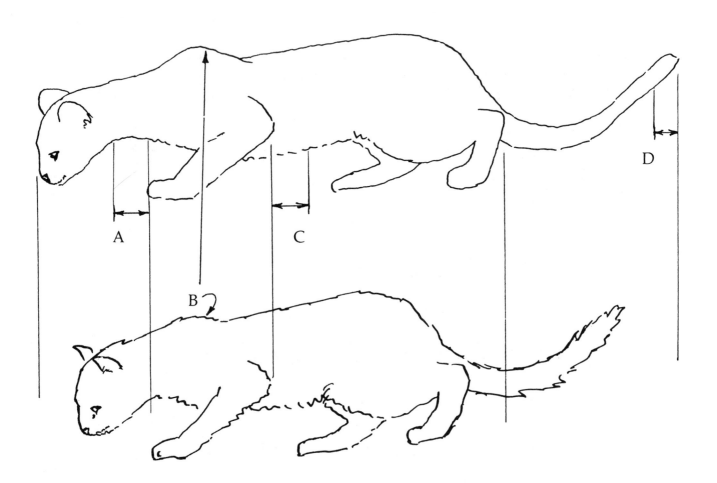

Figure 14–1
Comparison of the proportions of a margay and a house cat. (A) The margay's neck is longer. (B) The shoulders are shown lined up for this comparison. (C) The margay's body is longer. (D) The margay's tail is longer.

LESSON 54
Pen Drawing of a Margay

Tools and Materials
Fine-point pen; seventy-pound smooth or vellum-finish paper. (I used my 5×0 technical pen, which has an extremely fine point. A very fine crowquill point or a 3×0 technical pen will also do.)

Procedure
Follow the instructions in Chapter 2 to copy and transfer the outline drawing of the margay in figure 14–2 to your working paper.

Use the completed drawing, figure 14–3, to guide your work as you follow the step-by-step instructions accompanying figure 14–4 to complete your drawing. When you are drawing the dark outer edges of the spots, place your hatch marks very close together. When you are toning the light background color between the spots, however, space your hatch marks a little farther apart, and draw them right over the previously drawn marks. Be sure that you leave the white fur areas untouched.

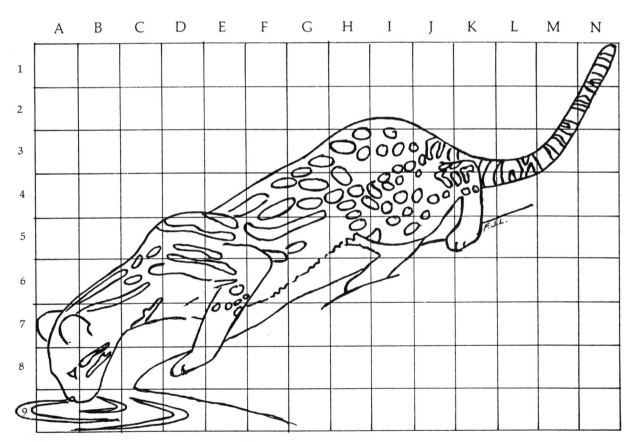

Figure 14–2
The composition outline and spot pattern of a margay.

Figure 14-3
A 5×0 technical pen drawing (a very fine point) of the margay.

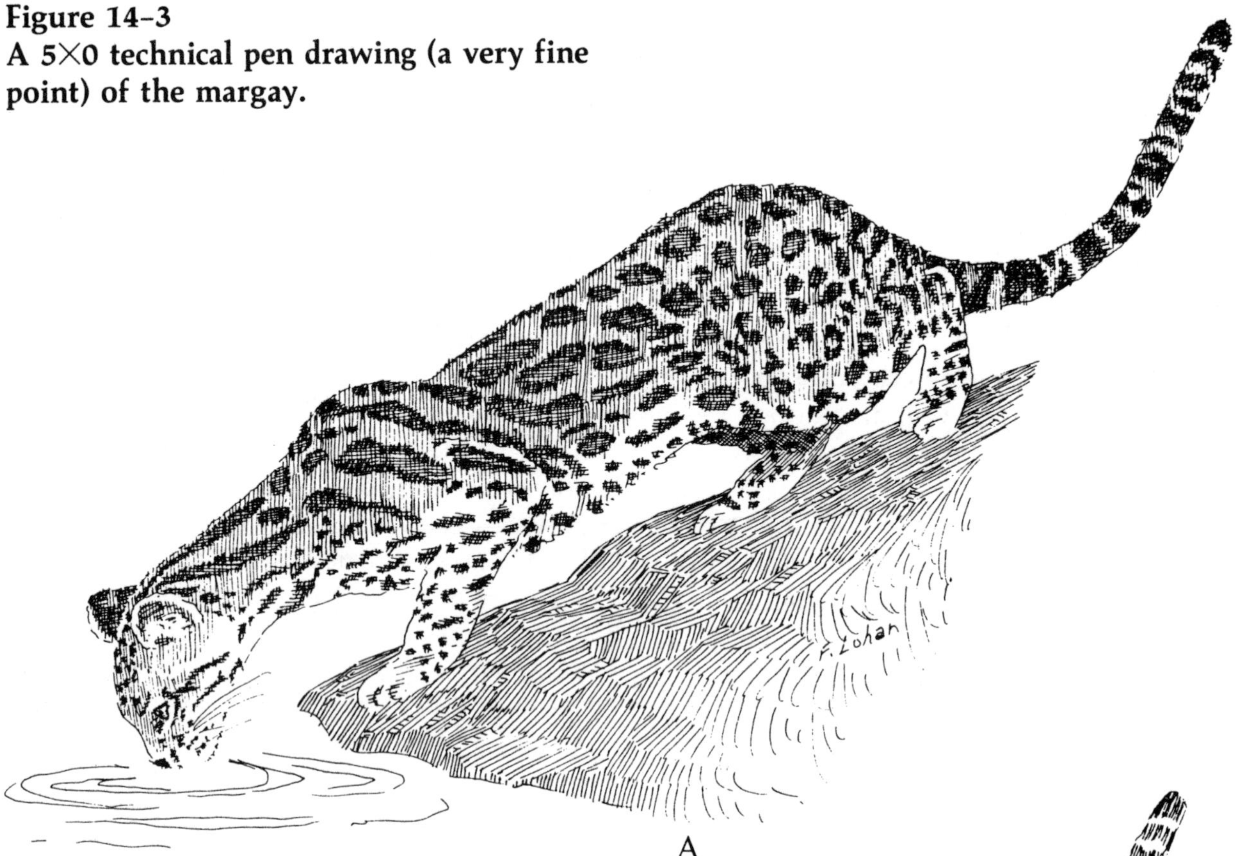

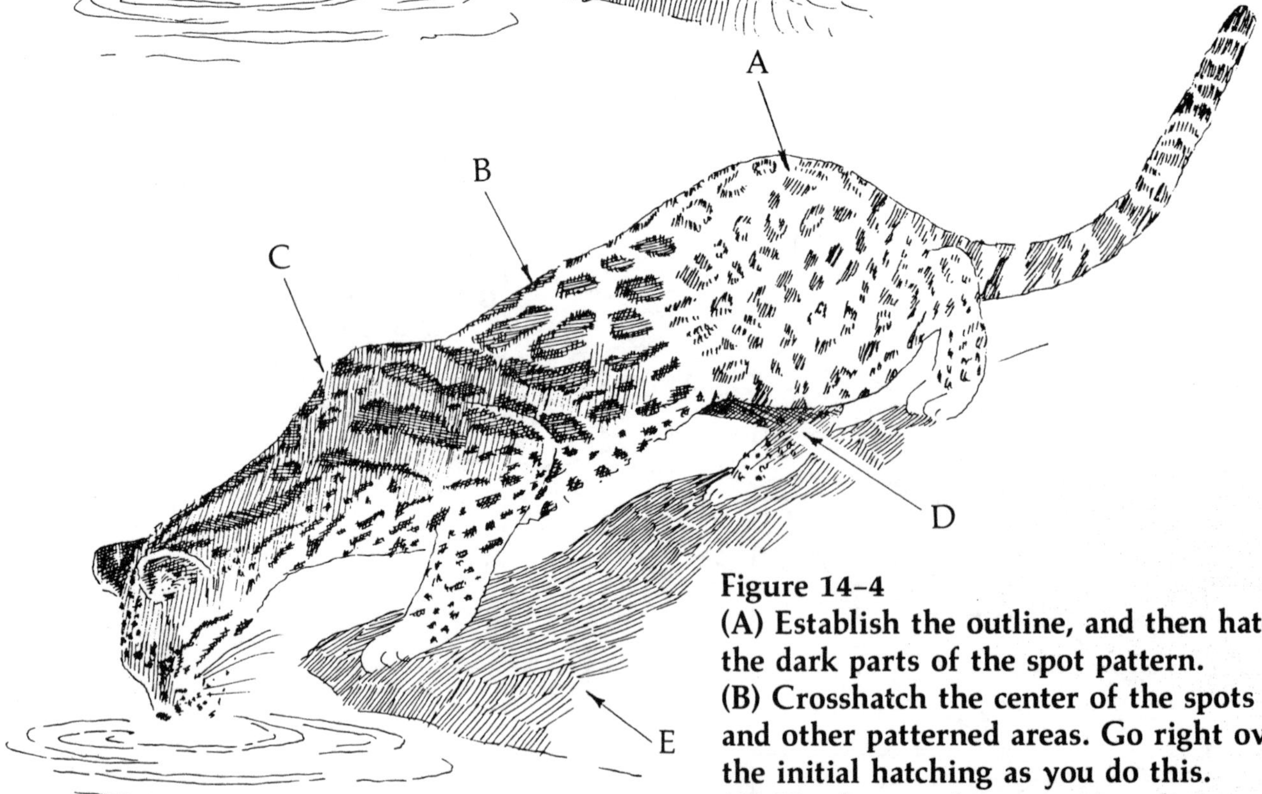

Figure 14-4
(A) Establish the outline, and then hatch the dark parts of the spot pattern.
(B) Crosshatch the center of the spots and other patterned areas. Go right over the initial hatching as you do this.
(C) Hatch over the entire toned area of the body, but leave the white parts of the fur untouched (refer to figure 14-3).
(D) Crosshatch the shaded leg. (E) Hatch the ground.

LESSON 55
Pencil Drawing of a Margay

Tools and Materials
Sharp HB and broad-point HB pencils; tracing vellum; kneaded eraser. (The tracing vellum is somewhat abrasive so it is possible to get very dark darks with almost any pencil. You will have to use the HB pencil very lightly to tone the lighter background color of the fur between the spots.)

Procedure
Place your tracing vellum directly on top of your composition outline (figure 14–2). You may want to use a paper clip or two to hold these sheets together while you work. The tracing vellum allows you to see right through to the image you are drawing; there will be no need to transfer the drawing because you are drawing on the final paper. Figure 14–5 shows the completed pencil drawing; use it to guide your work.

Follow the sequence shown in figure 14–6 to do your version of the margay, but be sure to use your pencil lightly when you tone the fur between the spots. If necessary, a touch or two with your kneaded eraser will lighten any places that you inadvertently make too dark.

Figure 14–5
An HB pencil sketch of the margay. This was done on tracing vellum, a somewhat abrasive surface that takes pencil very well.

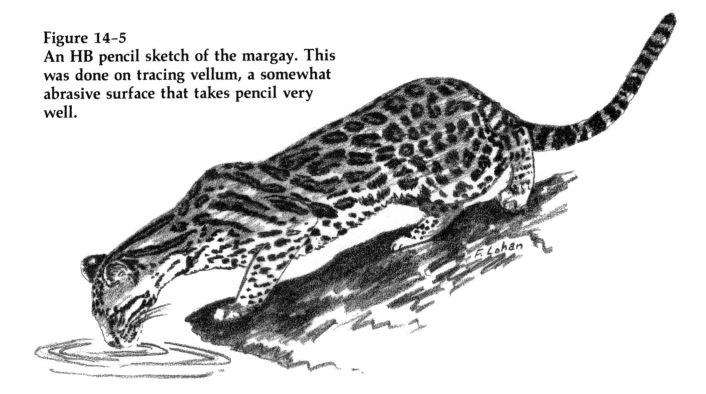

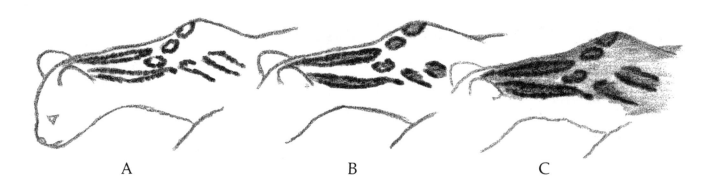

A   B   C

Figure 14–6
(A) Do the dark edges of the patterned areas. (B) Add the lighter interior parts of the patterned areas. (C) Tone the whole body, but leave the white fur areas untouched.

Figure 14–7
A pencil sketch of the margay on linen-finish paper.

LESSON 56
Pencil Drawing of a Margay on Linen-Finish Paper

Tools and Materials

Broad-point 6B, 3B, and HB pencils, and sharp B pencil; linen-finish paper; kneaded eraser. (Note that you can do this subject on plain vellum-finish paper just as well. The only difference will be the lack of the linen pattern in the dark passages.)

Procedure

Transfer a copy of the composition drawing, figure 14–2, to your working paper. See Chapter 2 for instructions if necessary.

Figure 14–7 shows the completed pencil drawing on linen-finish paper. Use this illustration to guide you in completing your own drawing.

When I made my drawing, the first thing I did was complete the animal by following the sequence accompanying figure 14–6. I used my 6B pencil for the dark outlines around the spots, my B pencil for the insides of the spots, and my HB pencil for the lightest toned areas of the fur. Since the dark background

requires a lot of graphite, I knew I would smear it around if I did the background first. Figure 14–8 shows my steps in completing the dark background and getting it tightly against the figure of the animal.

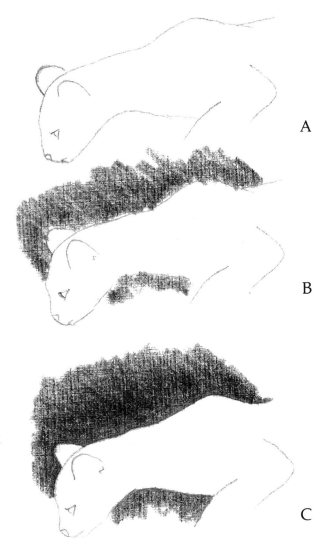

A

B

C

Figure 14–8
(A) Transfer the outline and complete the drawing of the animal with its fur pattern and shading, following the instructions accompanying figure 14–6.
(B) Rough in the dark background with a broad-point 6B pencil. (C) Trim the background tight against your outline by using a sharp 3B pencil.

LESSON 57
Pen Drawing of an Ocelot

Tools and Materials
Fine-point pen (I used my 3×0 technical pen); seventy-pound smooth or vellum-finish paper.

Procedure
Follow the instructions in Chapter 2 to copy and transfer the composition outline of figure 14–9 to your working paper.

Use figure 14–10, the completed pen sketch of the ocelot's head, to guide your work. Follow the steps accompanying figure 14–11 to bring your drawing to completion. It will take some careful pen work to give the whiskers the prominence they should have. Try to leave a little sliver of white paper just above each whisker, and bring your pen marks right up to the lower side of each whisker.

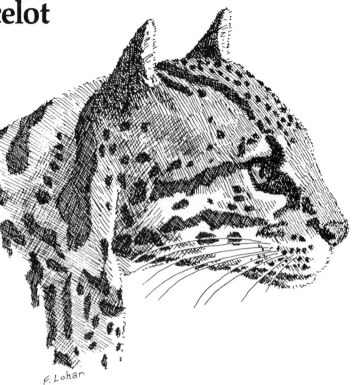

Figure 14–10
A 3×0 technical pen drawing of the ocelot's head.

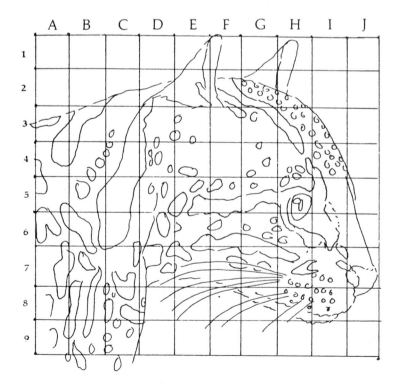

Figure 14–9
The composition outline and spot pattern for an ocelot's head.

A

Figure 14-11
(A) Establish the outline, and then hatch the spots. Erase the pencil guidelines when you no longer need them. (B) Crosshatch the spots to darken them. (C) Hatch over all of the toned areas of the fur, but be careful to leave the white patches on the face untoned. (D) Carefully crosshatch the eye, but leave a little white highlight. (E) Use hatch marks and dots on the nose. (F) Add the few shaded areas that give a little roundness to the sketch by hatching over what is already there.

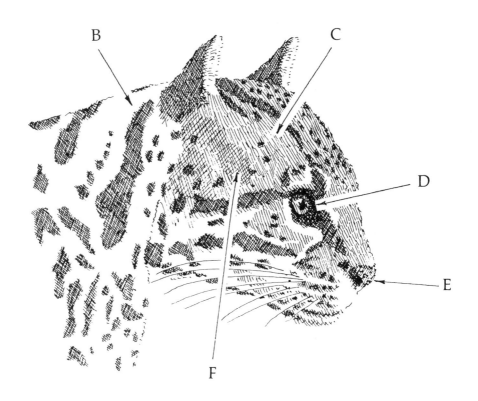

B   C

D

E

F

LESSON 58
Pen Sketch of a Jaguar

Tools and Materials

Fine-point pen; seventy-pound smooth or vellum-finish paper. (I used my 5×0 technical pen, although you can do this study using a very fine crowquill point or your 3×0 technical pen.)

Procedure

Follow the instructions in Chapter 2 to copy and transfer the outline drawing of figure 14–12 to your working paper. Because there are so many small spots on the jaguar, I have included figure 14–13 to assist you in placing the spots on the animal.

The completed pen drawing, figure 14–14, should be your guide as you work on your drawing of this subject.

The steps to follow to do your drawing accompany figures 14–15 and 14–16. Erase your pencil guidelines as soon as you no longer need them. This minimizes the smearing of the graphite.

Figure 14–12
The outline composition drawing of a jaguar.

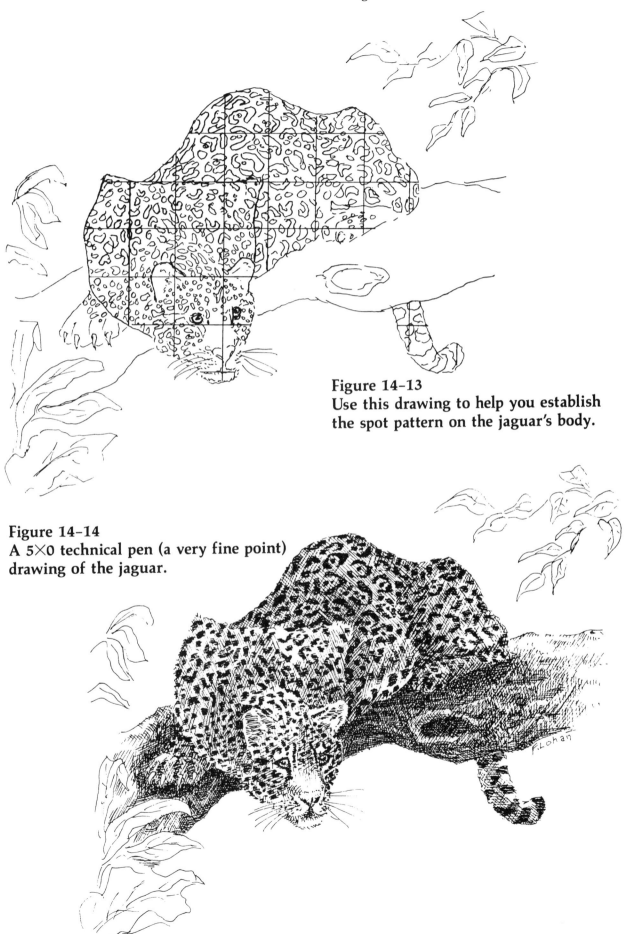

Figure 14–13
Use this drawing to help you establish the spot pattern on the jaguar's body.

Figure 14–14
A 5×0 technical pen (a very fine point) drawing of the jaguar.

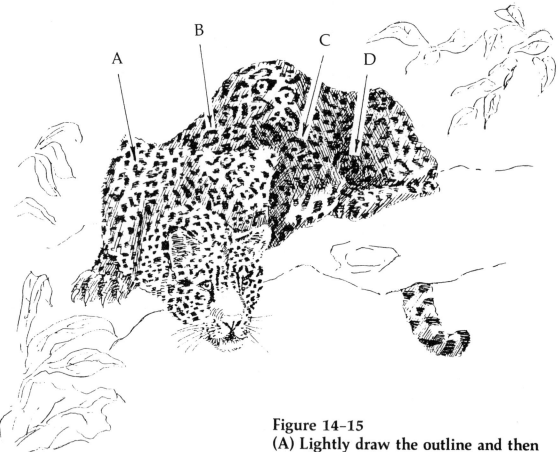

Figure 14-15
(A) Lightly draw the outline and then indicate the spot pattern with close hatch marks. Erase your pencil guidelines.
(B) Give the shaded areas one layer of hatching. Be sure to avoid the white facial and lip areas, the inside of the ears, and areas on the shoulders. (C) Apply the overall background fur tone by hatching over the entire animal except for the white areas mentioned in B. (D) Now hatch over those areas that must be darkened to give form and volume to the animal's body.

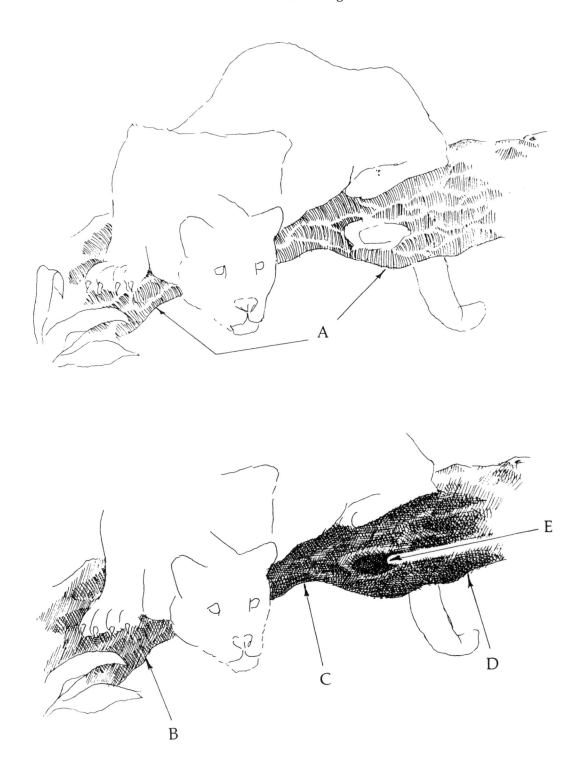

Figure 14-16
(A) Start the tree trunk with groups of hatch marks that are separated by white paper.
(B) Crosshatch over the tree trunk. (C) Crosshatch again wherever shadows fall on the tree trunk. (D) Add more crosshatching along the lower edge of the tree trunk to give it some roundness. (E) Make the knot hole very dark by crosshatching it.

LESSON 59
Pen Drawing of a Walking Jaguar

Tools and Materials
Fine-point pen (I used my 3×0 technical pen); seventy-pound smooth or vellum-finish paper.

Procedure
Copy and transfer the outline composition of figure 14–17 to your drawing paper, following the instructions in Chapter 2.

Use the completed drawing, shown in figure 14–18, to guide your work as you complete your drawing by following the instructions accompanying figures 14–19, 14–20, and 14–21.

Be careful as you do the mouth area because you want to leave the slivers of white paper alone where the whiskers cross the dark mouth. The grass and weed pattern and texture are suggested by a more or less continuous scribble line drawn with the pen.

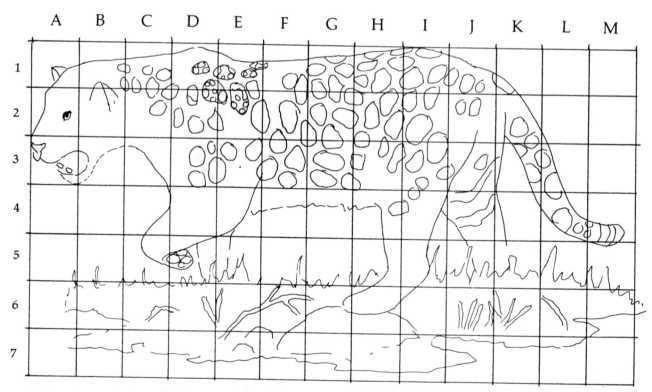

Figure 14–17
The composition outline and major spot pattern of a walking jaguar.

Figure 14-18
A pen drawing of a walking jaguar.

Figure 14-19
(A) Carefully tone the eye and the mouth. Try to leave white slivers across the dark of the mouth to suggest whiskers. (B) Hatch the small spots on the face and neck.
(C) Stipple the background fur tone, but leave a white sliver to separate the head from the ear.

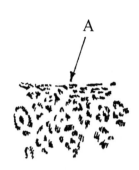

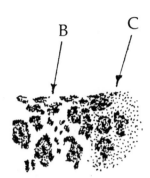

Figure 14-20
(A) Hatch the dark parts of the larger spots. (B) Stipple the darker centers of the larger spots. (C) Stipple the fur between the spots, but do not make it as dark as the fur in the middle of the large spots. If you see no distinction, darken the centers of the spots a little by adding more dots.

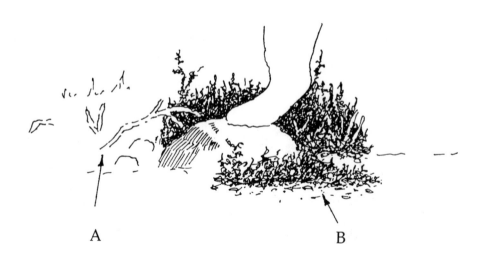

Figure 14-21
(A) Outline some of the light twigs and stones on the ground. (B) Ink in the grass and weed indications on the ground.

15
Sketching Polecats and Meerkats

Sketching a Polecat, or Skunk

Sketching a Standing Meerkat

Sketching a Group of Meerkats

As a diversion, this chapter includes a couple of animals that are not related to cats but that have "cat" or "kat" in their names. Practice your sketching on a polecat (or skunk) and some meerkats—South African relatives of the weasel.

LESSON 60
Sketching a Polecat, or Skunk

Tools and Materials
Broad-point 3B pencil; seventy-pound vellum-finish paper; kneaded eraser.

Procedure
Copy and transfer the outline drawing (figure 15–1) to your paper by following the instructions in Chapter 2.

Figure 15–2 shows the completed pencil sketch of a striped skunk. Using this figure as your guide, follow the instructions that accompany figure 15–3.

The object in this little study is to create the impression of fur with the main texturing strokes and to darken the light spaces that remain between these strokes to convey the idea of solid black, letting the fur strokes show through.

This is a very simple sketch, but as in the other lessons in this book, start with the eyes, nose, and ears and then proceed to the body of the animal.

Figure 15–1
The gridded outline of a striped skunk.

Figure 15–2
A quick 3B pencil study of
the striped skunk.

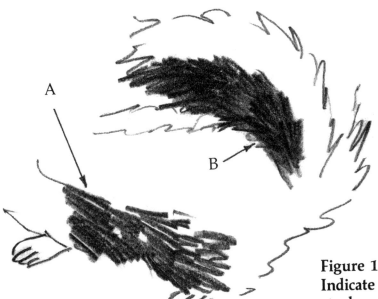

Figure 15–3
Indicate the black fur with individual
strokes of the broad-point 3B pencil. Let
most of the strokes show, as at A. Then
go over the black area lightly with the
same pencil to darken the white areas
that show between the strokes, as at B,
but let the strokes still show to suggest
fur.

LESSON 61
Sketching a Standing Meerkat

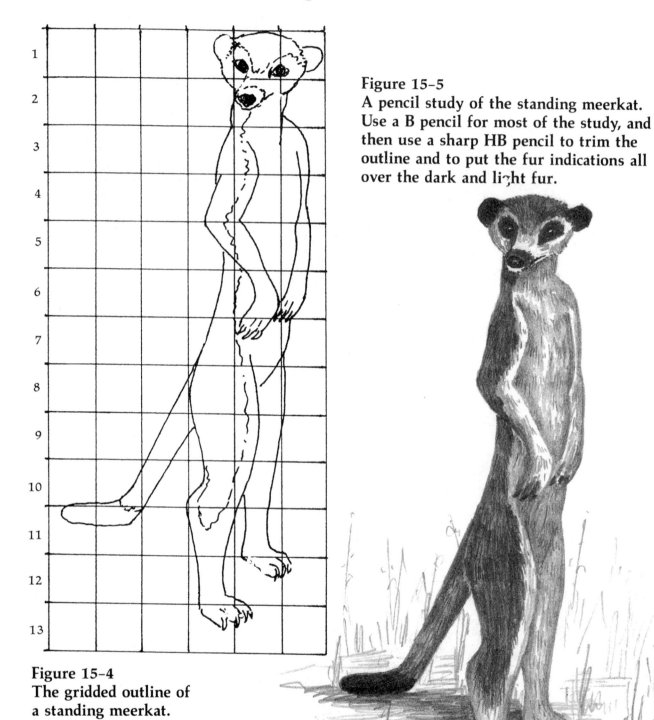

Figure 15-4
The gridded outline of
a standing meerkat.

Figure 15-5
A pencil study of the standing meerkat.
Use a B pencil for most of the study, and
then use a sharp HB pencil to trim the
outline and to put the fur indications all
over the dark and light fur.

Tools and Materials
Sharp HB and broad-point 3B and B pencils; seventy-pound vellum-finish paper; kneaded eraser.

Procedure
Follow the instructions in Chapter 2 to copy and transfer the outline in figure 15-4 to your paper.

Use the completed pencil drawing, figure 15-5, to guide you as you draw your own version of the subject. Do the eyes, nose, and mouth first, and then use a B pencil heavily to get the darks on the back and head; use it lightly for the lighter underparts and legs. Now use a sharp HB pencil to trim the edges of the figure and to superimpose some fur marks all over the meerkat's body. If an area gets a little too dark, press your kneaded eraser to the area to lighten it somewhat.

An even quicker study of the same subject is shown in figure 15-6. In this case I used just a 3B pencil, starting with the head area, as you see in figure 15-7. I trimmed the edges of the animal's body with the sharp edge of the broad-point 3B pencil by using it as shown in Chapter 1, figure 1-6, at right.

**Figure 15-6
A 3B pencil study of the meerkat.**

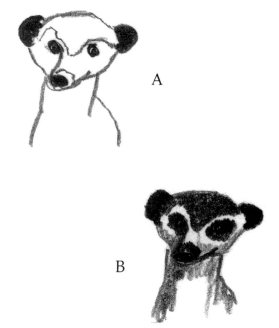

A

B

**Figure 15-7
(A) Use a 3B pencil to outline the meerkat and to indicate the eyes, ears, and nose. (B) Use the same 3B pencil to tone the black around the eyes and nose and to do the dark head. Use it more lightly to slightly tone the white fur areas.**

LESSON 62
Sketching a Group of Meerkats

Tools and Materials
Broad-point 3B pencil; seventy-pound vellum-finish paper; kneaded eraser.

Procedure
Copy and transfer the outline drawing in figure 15–8 to your paper, referring to the instructions in Chapter 2 if necessary.

Use the quick pencil sketch in figure 15–9 as a guide. Proceed as explained in the previous lesson; in this case, however, the drawing is smaller and you will need to show a little less detail with the pencil.

These last three lessons are examples of quick pencil studies in which detail is neglected and simple form, action, and tone are emphasized. If you were sketching animals from life, you would proceed this way because they would seldom sit still for you to create a good, time-consuming portrait. Such quick studies would then be used at your leisure at home to create more complete drawings, using the action you captured in the field and reference books to get the details of coloration and marking.

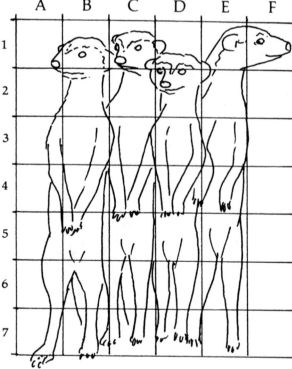

Figure 15–8
The gridded outline of a group of meerkats.

Figure 15–9
A quick 3B pencil study of the group of meerkats.

16
A Final Word on
Pen Techniques

Fountain Pens

Fine-Point Pen Work and Foreground
  Development

Fine-Point and Coarse-Point Pen Techniques

Reclining Lion

Fine Detail in Small Drawings

Fountain Pens

Today's fountain pens make it extremely easy to sketch with pen and ink almost any time and any place. For quite a few years I used to travel on business all over the United States, Europe, and Japan. I always had my artist's fountain pen and a number of blank 3″ × 5″ index cards in my jacket pocket to make quick studies at odd times. The 3″ × 5″ cards are stiff and take ink quite well. Naturally, a pencil also worked well for this purpose but the graphite had a tendency to smear because the cards rubbed together in my pocket. In later years I used some of the pen studies as the bases for lessons in some of my books.

The artist's fountain pen does not make a very fine line, even if it has a point called "extra fine." Technical drawing pens have extremely fine points when you get to the 3×0 (triple zero) or 5×0 (five zero) sizes. The makers of today's technical pens have pretty well solved the earlier problems of ink drying in the pen and clogging the extremely fine points, so now these instruments are as suitable for portable sketching as the more common fountain pen. This is something you might consider when you go on vacations or travel for other reasons.

Fine-Point Pen Work and Foreground Development

Figure 16-1 shows a 3×0 technical pen sketch of the head of a serval. Short hatch marks were used to tone the darker fur and the fur in the shade. The same technique was used in figure 16-2, a study of a meerkat's head. Compare the meerkat example with the pencil study in figure 15-7B. The use of short hatch marks in your line work will allow a little more delicate control of tones.

Figure 16-3 shows a partial study of a serval. It is the same composition as used in figures 12-6 and 12-9, and the same 3×0 technical pen was used in all cases. In the example here I used short hatch marks, and I developed the foreground vegetation completely. In the earlier examples in Chapter 12, I used longer hatch marks and did not attempt to develop the foreground. The method of showing grasses and small foliage in figure 16-3 is easy, but it takes some time to do. If there is much foreground you may spend more time drawing it than you do drawing the subject. In the earlier lessons I avoided any foreground

Figure 16-1
A fine-point pen study of a serval's head done with short hatch marks and fine crosshatching.

development so you would concentrate on the animal itself and the texturing necessary to suggest, for example, fur, stripes, and roundness. You can add foregrounds to any of the previous lessons. You will find that the time you spend to do the foreground will pay off in an attractive little drawing that looks finished.

Figure 16-2
A fine-point pen study of a meerkat's head.

Figure 16-3
A fine-point pen study of a serval. Compare this technique, which uses short hatch marks and includes an indication of foreground grass, with the pen studies in figures 12-6 and 12-9. In the latter figures, long hatch lines were used, and no attempt was made to develop the foreground detail.

Fine-Point and Coarse-Point Pen Techniques

Fine pen points can be employed to develop fine detail in small drawings by the use of short hatch marks (to tone areas) and by the stipple technique. The drawings of the reclining lion in figures 16-5 and 16-6 show these techniques on the animals as well as on the foreground. In each case there is good representation of detail because the fine point allows a number of strokes or dots to be used to build up individual features.

When a course point is used in small drawings, the lines or dots produced are large, and you cannot get enough of them together to develop fine features. The same lion composition is shown in figures 16-7A and 16-7B, in which a coarse-point pen was used to draw the same hatched and stippled studies as in figures 16-5 and 16-6. You can see that the fine features are much more indistinct because the coarse-point pen just is not suitable for use at this small scale. If detail is ignored, however, and just light and shadow emphasized, the coarse-point pen produces a very nice study, as you see in figure 16-7C. For this kind of representation at this size the coarse-point pen is more suitable than the fine-point pen.

Figure 16–5
A fine-point pen study of the reclining lion, including indication of the foreground grass.

Figure 16–6
A fine-point pen stipple study of the reclining lion. The fine dots allow some development of detail.

Figure 16–7
(A) A coarse-point pen study done in the manner of figure 16-5. Detail is less distinct with the coarse pen. (B) A coarse-point pen stipple drawing in the manner of figure 16-6. The large dots do not allow much detail to be represented. (C) A coarse-point pen study in which only shadows and highlights are rendered. This is a very effective use of the coarse-point pen at this scale of drawing.

LESSON 63
Reclining Lion

Tools and Materials
Fine-point pen (I used my 3×0 technical pen) and coarse-point pen (I used my artist's fountain pen); seventy-pound smooth or vellum-finish paper.

Procedure
Copy and transfer figure 16–4 to your paper, following the instructions in Chapter 2. Make two impressions, one on each of two different pieces of paper.

Use what you have learned from making the stipple and hatched drawings in previous lessons to do your own drawing of figure 16–5 or 16–6 with your fine-point pen on one of the transferred impressions. Try to get a grassy look to the foreground work. It may take a bit of practice to get it looking right, but once you have it you will see that it is quite easy to do.

Now take your coarse-point pen and use figure 16–7C to guide you in producing the simple black-and-white drawing. You will see how quickly this kind of study can be completed and how effective it is. This is a good approach for poster work.

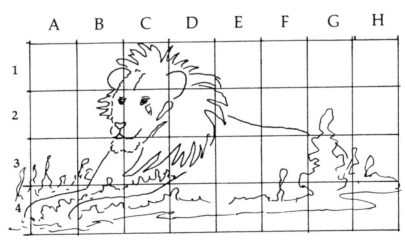

Figure 16–4
The gridded composition drawing of a reclining lion.

Fine Detail in Small Drawings

To get fine detail in small drawings you must consider reduction of larger drawings. Working large facilitates the development of detail, and working in an open manner will retain the detail, even under conditions of severe reduction in size. Figure 16–8 shows a partially completed study of a tiger's face. The drawing was done, as is shown in the full-size reproduction in figure 16–8A, with a relatively broad pen point—my artist's fountain pen. It was easy to do the whiskers at this size. Figure 16–8B shows a reduction to 30 percent of the full size (that is, thirty percent of the linear dimension—this is less than 10 percent of the original drawing area). Even using a fine-point pen it would be difficult to do a drawing the size of figure 16–8B and still get the sharp details, such as the whiskers, to be as clear as they are in the reduction.

Figure 16–8 (opposite page)
(A) A coarse-point pen study of part of a tiger's face. When a drawing is large the relatively large dots are quite capable of rendering detail, such as the whiskers, and gradations of tone, as under the tiger's eyes. (B) A reduction to 30 percent of the dimensions of the original drawing (less than 10 percent of the original area) preserves all the details. It would be difficult, or impossible, to clearly draw such detail at this small size, even with an extremely fine-point pen.

Other Books by Frank J. Lohan

Pen and Ink Techniques, Contemporary Books, Inc., Chicago, 1978, 96 pages.

This pen and ink sketching book for the beginner describes the materials required and gives ten basic step-by-step demonstrations as well as reference sketches covering a wide variety of subjects.

Pen and Ink Themes, Contemporary Books, Inc., Chicago, 1981, 106 pages.

This is a sketch-filled idea book that shows artists how to look around themselves to find sources of subject matter to sketch.

Pen and Ink Sketching Step by Step, Contemporary Books, Inc., Chicago, 1983, 130 pages, indexed.

Thirty-six step-by-step pen and ink demonstrations are included in this book. The subject matter covers barns, owls, raccoons, mountain lions, deer, ducks, songbirds, toads, stone lanterns, boats, and more.

Wildlife Sketching, Contemporary Books, Inc., Chicago, 1986, 240 pages, indexed.

Chapters on materials, drawing techniques, and basics of perspective introduce this book on how to sketch songbirds, trees, animals, flowers, mushrooms, water birds, reptiles, amphibians, and more. More than 600 individual drawings are included to show the artist how to draw each subject in pencil and in pen.

Countryside Sketching, Contemporary Books, Inc., Chicago, 1989, 260 pages, indexed.

How to sketch American and British countryside landscapes, mountain scenes, rural structures, and much more with the pen and the pencil. Fundamentals are included for sketching trees, rocks, buildings, lakes, waterfalls, mountains, ruined castles, ancient stone circles, homesteads, and more. More than 400 explanatory drawings show how you can draw such subjects.

Sketching Birds, Contemporary Books, Inc., Chicago, 1990, 144 pages, indexed.

After sections on tools and materials and drawing techniques, fifty-nine step-by-step lessons show the artist how to draw baby robins, sparrows, herons, ducks, geese, orioles, woodpeckers, sandpipers, ospreys, owls, hawks, and more with the pen and the pencil. A section on making your own notepaper from your drawings is included.

Index